The King Arthur Myth in
Modern American Literature

The King Arthur Myth in Modern American Literature

by Andrew E. Mathis

McFarland & Company, Inc., Publishers
Jefferson, North Carolina, and London

Library of Congress Cataloguing-in-Publication Data

Mathis, Andrew E. 1969–
   The King Arthur myth in modern literature / by Andrew E.
Mathis.
      p.   cm.
   Includes bibliographical references and index.
   ISBN 0-7864-1171-6 (softcover : 60# alkaline paper) ∞
 1. American fiction — 20th century — History and criticism.
 2. Arthurian romances— Adaptations— History and criticism.
 3. American fiction —19th century — History and criticism.
 4. Medievalism — United States— History — 20th century.
 5. Medievalism — United States— History —19th century.
 6. Arthurian romances— Appreciation — United States.
 7. American fiction — English influences.
 8. Knights and knighthood in literature.
 9. Kings and rulers in literature.
10. Great Britain — In literature.
11. Middle Ages in literature.
 I. Title.

PS374.A78 M38   2002   2001044620
853'.509351— dc21

British Library cataloguing data are available

Manufactured in the United States of America

Cover art: Paul Berenson (www.paulb.com), *A Connecticut Yankee in
King Arthur's Court*, oil on canvas, 24"x35", 1993.

McFarland & Company, Inc., Publishers
  Box 611, Jefferson, North Carolina 28640
    www.mcfarlandpub.com

For my parents

Acknowledgments

The completion of this book would not have been possible without the direction and support of Professor Josephine Hendin of New York University, who offered invaluable advice and made herself available beyond the call of duty. Thanks are also due to Professors Cyrus Patell and Christopher Collins for reading the manuscript and offering important insights on how it could be improved. Michele Mollo's help in proofreading the manuscript was extraordinary.

Prior to my stay at NYU, the guidance and recommendations of Professors Evan Radcliffe and Jaye Berman of Villanova University were inspirational, and I never would have reached this point without them. Equally inspirational has been the encouragement of Leslie Workman, Kathleen Verduin, David Metzger, and Richard Utz of *Studies in Medievalism*.

Portions of Chapter 3 appeared previously in *Clues: A Journal of Detection*, Vol. 18, No. 2, of 1997. I am grateful for the permission of the Popular Press of Bowling Green, Ohio, which publishes *Clues*, to reprint this material.

Contents

Introduction

"The queen! the queen! It was her Majesty's own gift," replied
the earl, still gazing into the depths of the gem. "She took it
from her finger, and told me, with a smile, that it was an heirloom from her Tudor ancestors, and had once been the property of Merlin, the British wizard, who gave it to the lady of
his love. His art had made this diamond the abiding-place of
a spirit, which, though of fiendish nature, was bound to work
only good, so long as the ring was an unviolated pledge of
love and faith, both with the giver and receiver. But should
love prove false, and faith be broken, then the evil spirit
would work his own devilish will, until the ring were purified
by becoming the medium of some good and holy act, and
again the pledge of faithful love. The gem soon lost its virtue;
for the wizard was murdered by the very lady to whom he gave
it."

"An idle legend!" said the countess.

Thus begins the tradition of the use of the Arthurian cycle of
mythology among major American writers. The reference to Merlin, the
magus of King Arthur's court, by Nathaniel Hawthorne in his 1843 short
story "The Antique Ring" is merely one of convenience. The theme of
the tale — that lies destroy love — could have been illustrated using any
variety of symbols, or even the same symbol without the Arthurian reference. In the tale as we have it, the ring is passed down from generation to generation, from one pair of famous lovers to another (ending
with Queen Elizabeth I and the Earl of Essex), and finally surfaces in
contemporary New England. What Hawthorne accomplishes by juxtaposing the legendary tale of Merlin and his treacherous lover with a true
story such as the affair of Elizabeth and Essex is the integration of fact
and fiction and, more importantly, myth and history.

This accomplishment forms one major trajectory of the use of

1

Arthurian myth and legends by American writers—the use of Arthuriana to critique historical or contemporaneous events and figures. Mark Twain's *A Connecticut Yankee in King Arthur's Court* sets out to attack a variety of *both* historical and contemporaneous targets. Twain's victims range from medieval culture itself—particularly as manifested in sixth-century England—to the American South, which embraced the romanticized version of this culture. More broadly, *Connecticut Yankee* reflects a literary *Kulturkampf* between England and the United States that was picked up in interwar America by detective writer Raymond Chandler. In the late twentieth century, Donald Barthelme essentially inverted Twain's use of the Arthurian myth, parachuting the whole court of Camelot into England during World War II rather than taking, for instance, a baby boomer and thrusting him back in time to perform a series of comparisons and contrasts. By continuing the use of the Arthurian cycle to make specific statements about actual events—here the early years of World War II in the European Theater—Barthelme carried forward the trajectory in American fiction first seen in Hawthorne's "Antique Ring."

This use of myth to address and critique historical events spread beyond the realm of literature and entered popular culture as early as Twain's own time. This was part of the general trend of medievalism seen in the formation of fraternal orders among working people in the late nineteenth century. For Twain this phenomenon would be most significant, as the medievalist orders directly influenced the organized labor movement. And, as John Steinbeck observed late in his own career, the tendency of Americans to dress up like knights for reasons of social as well as political unity endured long after the labor struggles of the 1880s.

The infiltration of the Arthurian myth into American culture for the purposes of political, social, and cultural critique came to a head during U.S. involvement in World War II, when both the right-wing extremists who sympathized with the rise of totalitarianism and the moderates and leftists who fought to defeat the Axis powers used elements of Arthuriana to advance their causes. On one hand, for example, Hal Foster's *Prince Valiant* comic strip showed medieval knights battling Nazis disguised as Huns; on the other hand, political extremist William Dudley Pelley formed a Galahad Press and Galahad College to spread and perpetuate the ideals of National Socialism.

The quintessential melding of the Arthurian mythos with American politics came with the presidency of John Fitzgerald Kennedy. With an administration popularly known (albeit perhaps posthumously) as Camelot, not to mention a Celtic (Irish-American) background, Kennedy was the closest that twentieth-century America came to dubbing a King Arthur to rule over it. With his good looks, valiant military record, and gift for oratory, Kennedy's persona elevated what could be called "presidential" into the realm of "regal." That Kennedy was assassinated after only a thousand days in the White House served only to strengthen the connection to the Arthurian cycle, and it may be that, despite all the scandals about Kennedy revealed after his death, no American president has left quite so formidable a legacy as JFK.

Three years after Hawthorne wrote "The Antique Ring," his American literary contemporary Ralph Waldo Emerson published three poems with Arthurian themes. Perhaps following Hawthorne's lead, Emerson limited his treatment of the Arthurian myth to the character of Merlin in "Merlin I," "Merlin II," and "Merlin's Song." Of course, Emerson was much better known as an essayist and philosopher of Transcendentalism, and he never wrote any fiction. In fact, even as a poet his status is minor; his philosophical influence on Walt Whitman was his most important contribution to American poetry. So it is perhaps strange to find Emerson reaching toward the same mythical influences as the fiction writers of his day, particularly Hawthorne, whose own philosophy was far removed from Emerson's. It should not be surprising, then, that Emerson put the mythical character of Merlin to a far different use than did Hawthorne.

For Emerson, the emphasis on Merlin is far more philosophical than for Hawthorne. As Emerson scholar and editor Stephen Whicher has written:

> Emerson refers not so much to the magician of Arthurian legend as to the reputed author of many traditional poems of the Welsh bards.... To Emerson the name meant a poet who sings with natural inspiration, as an Aeolian harp makes music, whose song is allied to wild and grand forces of nature, and who, above all, has a potency that will change the hearts of men and direct their actions [Emerson 506].

Thus Merlin could be a sort of Transcendentalist model and hero for Emerson. Note that, like Emerson's friend Henry David Thoreau, the Emersonian Merlin is tied to nature but is devoted to "chang[ing] the hearts of men." Thoreau's *Walden* stands as a prime example of these simultaneous but not competing expressions.

Out of Emerson's Merlin poems grows an aesthetic strand in American fiction that uses the Arthurian motif. While he may be best known and remembered for his political literature and reportage, John Steinbeck's Arthurian-themed fiction is notable for this vein. Nearly all of Steinbeck's novels make at least passing reference to the Arthurian legend in some way or another, and when they do, Steinbeck is often weighing the viability of the myth against its applicability to contemporary situations and finding that it comes up short. The recurrent conclusion in this more aesthetic tradition of Arthuriana in American fiction is that the myth no longer "works"; that is, that what was an ideal for the fifteenth century (when Thomas Malory wrote *Le Morte d'Arthur*) can no longer be understood as such or implemented in any similar form by a society living five centuries later.

Ironically, this is quite a different conclusion from the one Emerson seems to be suggesting by evoking Merlin in his poetry in the first place. But, as Whicher notes, Emerson isolated Merlin from the Malory depiction, whereas Steinbeck and most other American writers of Arthurian fiction do not. Steinbeck was less uniformly pessimistic about the myth's viability than were successors like John Gardner, but Steinbeck had a much longer career than Gardner did. Steinbeck is also one of the few writers of American Arthuriana who saw both the sociopolitical and aesthetic ramifications of the myth. However, the fascist Pelley was able to evoke Emerson's idea of the "Oversoul" in some of his mystical writings. This is yet another irony in the outcome of Emerson's role in introducing elements of Arthurian myth into the American literary tradition.

Another recurrence in the aesthetic tradition of Arthuriana in American fiction is debasement of aspects of the myth or of the myth as a whole. For Steinbeck, this may come in the form of the Holy Grail taking various shapes, such as a Geodetic Survey marker in *Tortilla Flat* or a family talisman in *The Winter of Our Discontent*, or less specifically in the failure of the myth to effect any sort of redemption on those who get caught up in it. Steinbeck's contemporary, Raymond Chandler, takes this myth debasement several steps further by picking apart the Arthurian myth — and even some of its own literary antecedents— and incorporating the basic elements into hard-boiled detective plots that include such seamy subjects as pornography and murder. A novel like *The Big Sleep* shows a society utterly incapable of being redeemed, as well as a knight errant near the end of his moral tether. Chandler, like Steinbeck, is not entirely apolitical in his application of the myth, but his politics are more literary than practical, and thus more in line with the aesthetic tradition. Through his use of non–Anglo-Saxon images and tropes, Chandler reasserts American authority in the detective fiction genre, first asserted by Edgar Allan Poe.

John Gardner, in his magnum opus *The Sunlight Dialogues*, seems closest to rendering the kind of Merlin that Emerson introduced to American literature. At the same time, the novel is a painstaking dissection of America in the late 1960s and early 1970s that shows the failure of the Arthurian myth, either via the figure of Merlin characterized as Gardner's Sunlight Man or the Camelot-type law and order that Gardner's protagonist tries and fails to apply to his situation. The Sunlight Man, misguided though he may be, fits Whicher's description of a character very much tied to nature but at the same time attempting to improve his fellow man. That he is simultaneously cast as a criminal and a fugitive is, on the one hand, a debasement of Arthurian myth, and, it could be argued, of Emerson's specific take on an Arthurian character. On the other hand, it is merely symptomatic of the debasement of American culture in general.

While there are certainly other recurrent motifs in the use of Arthuriana in American fiction, these two streams contain the most of what passes beyond the realm of the science fiction and fantasy aisle at the local bookstore and constitutes the American literary tradition. That fiction mirrors culture is a given; that the relationship works in reverse is something Oscar Wilde touched upon brilliantly by wondering whether, in fact, life imitated art more than the other way around. Fraternal orders such as the Knights Templar drew from early medieval myths and legends often tied in with the Arthurian myth. Lines from a Broadway musical became the signature theme and funeral dirge for a tragic figure from American history. There are beach towns in New Jersey and California called Avalon. King Arthur arrived early on America's shores, and dwells here still.

CHAPTER I

Mark Twain

As the first piece of significant, lengthy Arthurian fiction produced in the United States, Mark Twain's *A Connecticut Yankee in King Arthur's Court* introduced several themes that would become inseparable from future Arthurian efforts by American writers. Twain used the Arthurian myth to express a form of literary nationalism; specifically, the author is voicing a point of view that attacks the United Kingdom, its monarchy, and its writers. By lampooning the Arthurian form rather than imitating it, Twain established a decidedly anti-medievalist style — an aspect of American Arthuriana that would reappear. Twain also detailed the dichotomy of views on medievalism in his own country, and he used Arthuriana to illustrate differences that remained between Northern and Southern society following the Civil War and Reconstruction. Also prominent in *Connecticut Yankee* is the politicization of the myth — the setting up of a narrative structure in which the Arthurian story not only stands on its own as a representation of an unfair, feudal society, but also is a symbol for destructive political currents in Twain's own time.

Twain did not begin writing *A Connecticut Yankee* intending it to be an attack on England. However, there is evidence that during the course of composing the novel, which he wrote between 1886 and 1889, Twain became aware of a criticism of American society by the British critic and poet Matthew Arnold, with whom Twain had become familiar through his longtime association with William Dean Howells. In *My Mark Twain*, Howells describes Arnold's coming to Howells' home in Boston and, not finding Howells there, asking his family where he could be found. When Arnold was told that Howells was with Twain in Hartford, Connecticut, Arnold replied, "Oh, but he doesn't like *that* sort of thing, does he?" (Howells *My*). The three writers were together at a reception for Arnold in Hartford during that same visit to the United

States. After talking with Twain, Arnold remarked to a friend, "Is Mark Twain never serious?" ("Real").

When Arnold subsequently published his essay "Civilisation in the United States," it was difficult not to see it as an attack on Twain. The essay is primarily concerned with how America differs from England in terms of arts, humanities, and society. Among Arnold's observations is the assertion that "of the really beautiful in the other arts, and in literature, very little has been produced there as yet" (Arnold 496). Addressing the lack of "distinction" here, Arnold writes, "The glorification of 'the average man,' who is quite a religion with statesmen and publicists there, is against it [distinction]. The addiction to 'the funny man,' who is a national misfortune there, is against it" (Arnold 497-98).

Shortly after the essay appeared, Howells wrote to Twain asking him to offer a rebuttal to Arnold. The first indication of Twain's displeasure with Arnold came in a letter from Twain to the president of Yale University in June 1888 accepting an honorary degree. Twain writes, "Arnold rather sharply rebuked the guild of American 'funny men' in his latest literary delivery, and therefore your honorable recognition of us is peculiarly forcible and timely" (Letter). Arnold was still on Twain's mind two years later — after the publication of *Connecticut Yankee* — when he gave a speech at a dinner in Boston entitled "On Foreign Critics" and explicitly accused Arnold of classism.

According to John B. Hoben, Twain's manuscript of *Connecticut Yankee* had been languishing, but Arnold's attack on America "provided an inner drive" for Twain to continue writing (Hoben 342). Marcus Cunliffe supports the theory that it was Arnold's essay that poisoned Twain's pen and adds that Twain had also been reading the radical Englishman George Standring's *People's History of the English Aristocracy*, which insists that "hereditary privilege was a fatal impediment to the development of democracy in Britain" (Cunliffe 1503). The outcome is a broad attack on England's national mythology, the Arthurian tales. This is a particularly convenient mode of attack since Arnold had himself composed Arthurian poetry, notably "Tristram and Iseult." We should note that Twain's ensuing attack was not intended to be a wholesale attack on English culture in the spirit of Arnold's essay. Instead, Twain intended to limit his criticisms to the monarchy and upper classes. Despite this note of fairness on Twain's part, however, the English were offended nonetheless (Paine 338). Twain had been an Anglophile up to this point, but the publisher's prospectus for *Connecticut Yankee*, which Twain likely approved, was unwavering in its attack on monarchy in general and England in particular: "The book answers the Godly slurs that have been cast at us for generations by the titled gentry of England. It is a gird at Nobility and Royalty, and makes the most irreverent fun of these sacred things" (Smith *Development* 167).

Connecticut Yankee appears to respond to Arnold's essay and England's inherent societal flaws in several places. For example, Arnold writes of American newspapers, "The absence of truth and soberness in them, the poverty in serious interest, the personality and sensation-mongering, are beyond belief" ("Civilisation" 498). Turning to the novel, in Chapter X, "Beginnings of Civilization," Hank Morgan sets Clarence, the page, to the task of journalism: "Of late I had been training him for journalism, for the time seemed about right for a start in the newspaper line; nothing big, but just a small weekly for experimental circulation in my civilization-nurseries" (*Yankee* 52).

Twain had spent his youth working in a series of newspaper jobs, and much of his time and effort during the period of the novel's composition was dedicated to his massive financial investment in the Paige Company's prototype for an automatic typesetter. Therefore, it is little wonder that Hank would fancy himself a newspaper man. Like Arnold, Hank sees a connection between journalism and civilization. However, Hank is less than pleased at Clarence's work, noting, "Yes, it was too loud. Once I could have enjoyed it and seen nothing out of the way about it, but now its note was discordant. It was good Arkansas journalism, but this was not Arkansas" (*Yankee* 149). What Twain seems to be implying is that the English are less adept at journalism than Americans; Clarence is, after all, English. Also significant is Twain's juxtaposition in this chapter of the first newspaper and the phenomenon of the king's evil, a form of tuberculosis common in the Middle Ages that was commonly "treated" by having the king lay his hands on those affected. In unifying the themes of journalism and medieval medicine, Twain lumps together the perceived English journalistic ineptitude and the inanities he believed were inherent in monarchism and established religion. This point of view is also evident when the monks who see Hank reading the newspaper call it a "dark work of enchantment" (*Yankee* 152).

Twain had learned of the king's evil by way of W.E.H. Lecky's *History of European Morals and History of England in the Eighteenth Century*, one of several historical readings Twain undertook while composing the novel. Another of Lecky's contributions is the hanging scene in Chapter XXXV, in which a young mother is hanged for stealing to provide for her infant, whom she clutches as she writhes in the noose (J.D. Williams 372-73). Through these examples, we are reminded of several of Twain's primary targets: the established Church, the exploitation of the poor, and the concept of the aristocracy, summed up by Hank when he states, "[Just] as in the remote England of my birth-time, the sheep-witted earl who could claim long descent from a king's leman, acquired at second-hand from the slums of London, was a better man than I was" (*Yankee* 43). Twain, via Hank, equates sixth-century England with nineteenth-century England in regard to classism.

Twain also turned to Hippolyte Taine's *L'Ancien Regime* for historical observations when constructing the novel. Rodney O. Rogers has linked the following passage — on the combined power of the medieval church and the state to tax the farmers — to a passage on French feudalism in Taine (Rogers 438):

> [F]irst the Church carted off its fat tenth, then king's commissioner took his twentieth, then my lord's people made a mighty inroad upon the remainder; after which, the skinned freeman had liberty to bestow the remnant in his barn, in case it was worth the trouble; there were taxes, and taxes, and more taxes, and taxes again, and yet other taxes — upon this free and independent pauper, but none upon his lord the baron or the bishop, none upon the wasteful nobility or the all-devouring Church ... [Twain *Yankee* 65].

Notably, Rogers points out that Twain originally had written a version of these lines for inclusion in *A Tramp Abroad*. After excising the section from *Tramp*, Twain added the slights to the established church. We can therefore assume that England's church shares the blame, in Twain's eye, for medieval social injustices. In fact, one of the sizable portions of *Connecticut Yankee* lifted directly from Malory — the scene of Lancelot slaying two giants that appears in the "Word of Explanation" preceding Chapter I — is used by Twain, according to David Ketterer, to symbolize the dual enemies of monarchy and the established church (Ketterer, "Apocalypse" 420).

Twain's attacks on England's established church also come in the form of Calvinism. Twain had been raised a Presbyterian, so it's little wonder that Hank is Presbyterian also. In Chapter X, Hank contemplates the overthrow of the church, stating, "I could have given my own sect the preference and made everybody a Presbyterian without any trouble ..." (*Yankee* 50). Twain also had great admiration for Oliver Cromwell, who led the Parliamentarians and Puritans of England to overthrow Charles I and establish a commonwealth. In fact, Twain was a direct descendant of Geoffrey Clement, one of the judges who sentenced Charles I to death, and he often bragged about it, when in the right company (Sargent 23-26).

Twain's admiration of Cromwell is first manifested in *Connecticut Yankee* in the bullet-hole in the armor on display at Warwick castle that serves as a framing device for the novel. Hank muses that the bullet hole may have been caused "maliciously by Cromwell's soldiers" (*Yankee* 6). Elsewhere, Hank evokes Cromwell less directly in expressing his desire that England, after Arthur, should become a republic (*Yankee* 229). In a related vein, on the eve of the publication of *Connecticut Yankee*, Twain made reference in a letter to Howells to a passage from the forthcoming novel — unfortunately expurgated in the extant editions — that remarks very favorably on the French Revolution (Twain and Howells 613-14). Years later, Twain would write with enthusiasm about republican revolutions in South America (Twain and Howells 621-23; 626-27).

Beyond responding to Arnold's criticisms and attacking what he saw as the corrupt institutions of monarchy and state religion, Twain also gave a beating to the entire medieval culture of chivalry, and it is here that *Connecticut Yankee*'s attacks on England and the American South begin to overlap. Not by coincidence, Twain had been given his first copy of Malory's *Morte d'Arthur* by the Southern writer George Washington Cable, with whom he had gone on lecture tours. As Cable was a friend, he is not a target of Twain's pen. However, an important target for Twain is Sir Walter Scott, not only because he frequently wrote within a medieval framework, but also because of the popularity of his work in the American South long after his death in 1832.

Scott's work was pivotal in transplanting the chivalric tradition to the South, where the model was copied not only in a class context but in a racial context as well. Chivalry, to the post–Civil War South, implied the protection of white women from the perceived rape hazard represented by free black men. Twain and others believed the consequent lynchings and the sustained practice of racial segregation could be attributed in part to the continued chivalric tradition. Twain had already made his feelings about Scott very clear in *The Adventures of Huckleberry Finn*, the novel immediately preceding *Connecticut Yankee* in the Twain canon, wherein the steamboat *Walter Scott* is destroyed by an explosion on the Mississippi. The clear racial theme of that novel provides a context for understanding Twain's belief in Scott's culpability in the perpetuation of racial inequity.

The hostility toward Scott continues in *Connecticut Yankee*. For instance, there is the simple predilection of Hank to exclaim "Great Scott!" whenever he is presented with a particularly ridiculous medieval situation. More directly, Hank pokes fun at Scott's most beloved work when he observes the profanity of the common Arthurian-era Englishman and attacks Scott's sanitization of history:

> Suppose Sir Walter, instead of putting the conversations into the mouths of his characters, had allowed them to speak for themselves? We should have had talk from Rachel and Ivanhoe and the soft lady Rowena which would embarrass a tramp in our day. However, to the unconsciously indelicate all things are delicate. King Arthur's people were not aware that they were indecent, and I had presence of mind enough not to mention it [Twain *Yankee* 26].

Other implications against Scott and the chivalric tradition are couched in criticisms by Twain against his own time. For instance, the two scenes mentioned above with respect to Lecky's influence on the novel — the exploitation of the farmers and the hanging of the young mother — can both be seen as reflections on the plight of Southern sharecroppers, who were largely African-American, and on Southern lynchings.

Twain expands on the theme of the innate inequities of monarchy and chivalry through the use of comparison — which is also the source of most of the novel's humor. *Connecticut Yankee* is a fish-out-of-water story, with the fish becoming a better air-breather than his counterparts. Howard Baetzhold cites a letter from Twain to a correspondent that says his forthcoming novel was "not going to be 'a satire peculiarly' but 'more especially a *contrast*' [emphasis Twain's] between the daily life of the time & that of today" (Baetzhold 344). Years later, in his autobiography, Twain reiterated this sentiment.

> [*Connecticut Yankee*] was an attempt to imagine ... the hard conditions of life for the laboring and defenseless poor in bygone times in England, and incidentally contrast these conditions with those under which the civil and ecclesiastical pets of privilege and high fortune lived in those times. I think I was purporting to contrast that English life of the ... Middle

Ages, with the life of modern Christendom and modern civilization ... [Twain *Autobiography* 271].

Twain achieved this contrast on two levels. One is through the use of contemporaneous popular-culture items—for example, the beginnings of Chapters XVI and XX, with their images of knights wearing placards hawking products like "Persimmons's Soap" and "Peterson's Prophylactic Tooth-Brush" (Twain *Yankee* 78; 99). Similarly, the dubbing of Hank and Alisande's daughter "Hello-Central"—that being the standard greeting of early telephone operators—is a nod to the vernacular of Twain's (and Hank's) own age.

Elsewhere, Twain is able to force observation of inequality on the part of his sixth-century characters, as when King Arthur and Hank travel the countryside incognito. Interestingly, Arthur is a somewhat sympathetic character who seems inherently less responsible for the prejudices and inequities of the system than the average monks or knights. Notably, Arthur himself is captured and his life put at risk by the system of which he is the figurehead. Even the king cannot ultimately escape the injustices of the monarchical system.

While Queen Victoria, Britain's monarch when *Connecticut Yankee* was published, is not represented in the novel, her poet laureate, Alfred Lord Tennyson, is. Tennyson's *Idylls of the King* were also considered instrumental in continuing the chivalric tradition in England and the American South, including the negative aspects of that tradition. The skewering comes in the form of Daniel Beard's illustrations of Merlin the magician using Tennyson as the model (Twain *Yankee* 22).

Beard's own place in the field of Arthuriana in his subsequent career is interesting. As one of the founders of the Boy Scout movement in America, Beard had a close relationship with Lord Robert Baden-Powell, who founded the original Scouting movement in Britain in the first decade of the twentieth century. Baden-Powell was a devotée of the Arthurian myth, and in his scouting handbooks he included tales about the Knights of the Round Table. The Arthurian influence on scouting was also felt in the U.S., with one early (1915) scouting organization dubbed the Knights of King Arthur. Beard, however, wanted to imbue American Scouts with indigenously American myth and folklore:

> I confined myself to the United States for my inspiration. I did not summon to my aid King Arthur and his Round Table, the glistening armor of the tourney, Richard the Lionhearted,

the Black Prince or Saladin of the Saracens. No, not even
Robin Hood, though he was more my type of man. In place
of the lance and buckler was the American long rifle and
buckskin clothes, in place of the shining plumed helmet was
the American coonskin cap, the tail of the 'coon its plume
[Beard 353-54].

Beard's attitude toward medieval myth and its British proponents
is obvious in *Connecticut Yankee*'s illustrations. Merlin, with the visage
of Tennyson, is by far the most maligned character in the entire novel
(though he does get the last laugh), as he is defanged repeatedly by Hank
and his superior Yankee "magic." Just as an attack on the Arthurian legend is really a strike against England by attacking its national mythology, so was lampooning Tennyson since, when *Connecticut Yankee*
appeared, Tennyson was the poet laureate and therefore a convenient
symbol of the realm.

While it should be emphasized that Twain did not direct Beard in
his models for his work, he nonetheless requested no revisions of Beard's
work and found that it was well-suited to his novel. In a letter of grat-
itude to Beard he wrote, "There are a hundred artists who could have
illustrated any other of my books, but only one who could illustrate this
one. It was a lucky day I went netting for lightning bugs and caught a
meteor. Live forever" (Beard 337-38). As Henry Nash Smith and William
M. Gibson conclude, "The two men were united at this time in their
enthusiasm for a vague but deeply felt political program: the struggle of
the common man against the princes and rulers of this world (especially
the British aristocracy) for the right to work and to govern himself eco-
nomically as well as politically" (Twain and Howells 611).

Beard's illustrations make plain many of Twain's implicit assump-
tions about the similarities between the sixth century and the nineteenth
century with regard to inequality. For instance, one of Beard's principal targets was financier Jay Gould, whose likeness Beard chose for the
face of a slavedriver (Twain *Yankee* 204). In another less specific but no
less pointed illustration, Beard presents a triptych of drawings, each
involving an authority figure lording it over a subordinate with the cap-
tion "Brother! — To dirt like this?" and the means of subjugation labeled
"Oppression" (Twain *Yankee* 160). The first drawing, which represents
the sixth century, shows a king and a serf with the means of oppression
being a sword. The second drawing is a slave master and a black man in
chains, with oppression symbolized by a law book. The final drawing is

a financier and a wage-laborer, with money being the key instrument of oppression. Notably, in each drawing, the face of the superior is the same, representing the continuing inequities of society in both Britain and America. Notable also is Beard's illustration of the concept of protection, discussed below, which features a fat vulture symbolizing industry beside a starving dog labeled "Labor" (Twain *Yankee* 185).

This is not to suggest that Twain did not also offer direct indictments of nineteenth-century worker exploitation by America's so-called robber barons. Indeed, Twain most prominently dubbed his Yankee "Morgan," a name that resonates on both medieval and contemporary levels. On the one hand, like Malory's Morgan le Fay, Hank Morgan is a magician of sorts, mesmerizing and striking fear in the hearts of the populace of Camelot. Hank does not practice "real magic," but as Peter Messent points out, "the power associated with the figure of scientist/inventor is often, in the popular imagination, linked with destructive potential" ("Towards the Absurd" 179). On the other hand, Morgan was also the surname of a family of American bankers and war profiteers who were thought to exploit the working class to the same extent as Gould. Henry Nash Smith cites a late entry in Twain's notebook that states, "MORGAN consolidates steel, cooper, cable, ships, the WORLD's commerce — Europe began to decline" (Smith *Fable* 94).

Even the choice of Morgan's first name is meaningful: Hank is the nickname for Henry — the most common name of kings of England at Twain's time, the last of whom was a terrible despot and upon whose death, according to Twain's earlier novel *The Prince and the Pauper*, the people exclaimed, "The reign of blood is ended!" (57).

Furthermore, the nickname Morgan bestows on himself — "The Boss" — is rife with implications. The epithet reeks of corruption, particularly that of Boss Tweed of New York's Tammany Hall, who was in cahoots with Jay Gould (Shanley & Stillman 61). If it is true that power corrupts and that absolute power corrupts absolutely, we can apply this rule not only to Gould, Henry VIII, or J.P. Morgan, but to Hank Morgan himself. Smith points out that, throughout most of the novel, Hank is unable to fully exercise his power as the King's second-in-command; when he does, violence almost always ensues (Smith *Fable* 89). Shanley and Stillman concur, pointing out that, even though Hank seeks to eliminate exploitation, he ends up slaughtering the Knights of the Round Table to do so (Shanley and Stillman 278). In the words of James Cox, "Morgan becomes a grotesque caricature of the enlightenment he advocates" (Cox 392). This is just one inconsistency in Hank that affects the novel's ending.

The corruption of Hank reaches the most personal level of his character. He goes out of his way to humiliate the common man, as seen in Chapters XXXII and XXXIII, in which Hank debates the blacksmith Dowley over the issue of protection. Hank is not content merely to humiliate the man, so he threatens him with capital punishment (Shanley & Stillman 280). It is important to note that overt threats of violence, and even violence carried out, such as the hangings, ordered by Hank, of a band of talentless musicians in Chapter XVII and of Sir Dinadan, King Arthur's fool, for telling bad jokes in Chapter XL, show Hank's inability to maintain the chivalric code of behavior under the circumstances he faces.

The culmination of this inability comes in the Battle of the Sand Belt, the execution of which goes completely against the style of warfare described in Malory, wherein one knight challenges another knight, there is the allowance of preparation by both knights, and then battle ensues in the form of jousting, de-horsing, and then finally hand-to-hand combat. Instead of following Malory's example, Hank sits behind an electric fence and picks off knights with explosive artillery. If Malory's form of warfare is at the heart of the chivalric tradition, then in violating this norm Twain violates the entire chivalric code. The process is less grave but no less significant when Hank changes the Round Table from a symbol of knightly chivalry to a rudimentary stock exchange (Smith *Fable* 104).

Since Hank is the principal agent of change in *Connecticut Yankee*, we must look to him to answer our questions about the politics of the novel. Indeed it is important to remember that Twain appears in the novel only as an auxiliary narrator, and it is the character of Hank who criticizes the society in which he awakens (Shanley and Stillman 274). In Chapter XXXIII, "Sixth Century Political Economy," Hank argues with citizens of the realm of King Bagdemagus against the economic principle of protection, which guarantees a specific wage to each worker regardless of the desires of the employer (or employee). This would seem to be a conservative argument in favor of free trade. However, Hank shows his opponents how protection can eventually lead to higher wages and worker empowerment:

> The masters are these: novels, rich men, the prosperous generally. These few, who do no work, determine what pay the

vast hive shall have who do work. You see? They're a combine — a trade union, to coin a new phrase — who band themselves together to force their lowly brother to take what they
choose to give. Thirteen hundred years hence — so says the
unwritten law — the 'combine' will be the other way, and then
how these fine people's posterity will fume and fret and grit
their teeth over the insolent tyranny of trade unions [*Yankee*
190]!

Protection was a political issue in Twain's day, and one that put him, during Democrat Grover Cleveland's first bid for re-election, on the side of
the incumbent, who also was against protection. Earlier in his life, Twain
had been a Republican, mainly because of that party's foundation in the
abolition movement. But as Kenneth Lynn has pointed out, Twain left
the G.O.P. because of their too pro-business stance ("Volcano" 383). Hank
cleverly slips the mention of unions into his speech, but in a decidedly
unsocialistic manner, he casts them in a negative light, first calling the cor-
rupted owners of capital a "trade union" and then casting the vengeful
trade unions of the future as tyrannical. Essentially, he is suggesting how
unions may be avoided in the future by abolishing protection now.

Twain was increasingly politicized through his friendship with
Howells, who had been a keen supporter of Twain's idea for *Connecticut
Yankee* since its inception. "That notion of yours about the Hartford man
waking up in King Arthur's time is capital," Howells wrote to Twain,
using a clever monetary metaphor (Twain & Howells 550). Henry Nash
Smith, who edited the Howells-Twain correspondence for publication,
entitled the section of primarily political letters "Theoretical Socialists,"
concluding that Howell's rather overt socialist leanings had an effect on
his correspondent (Twain and Howells 581). Howells was later forced to
admit that, as Louis Budd has written, "[from] the vantage point of a mild
socialism ... his friend 'had not thought out any scheme for [righting]
the economic wrongs we abound in'" ("Uncle Sam" 405). Smith agrees,
stating that Twain, like most centrists of his day, was a "laissez-faire lib-
eral" (Smith *Fable* 90).

Nonetheless, Howells did exert some philosophical influence on his
friend, sometimes through encouragement of his fiction and sometimes,
as we have seen before in the case of Arnold's essay, through direct peti-
tioning. Another subject Howells suggested to Twain — one that would
become central to *Connecticut Yankee*— was that of the so-called Haymarket
riots of 1886 and their effect on the American labor movement and on
the Knights of Labor in particular.

The Noble and Holy Order of the Knights of Labor was founded in Philadelphia on Dec. 9, 1869, as a trade union to serve workers in all areas of industry. The use of the term "Knight" in the union's name came not only from predecessor groups such as the Knights of St. Crispin, a cobblers' union, but also from the background in Freemasonry and other secret societies that the founding members all shared. Among the original group were members of the Grand Army of the Republic, Improved Order of Red Men, the Royal Arcanum, and the Order of the Golden Cross. The union's first leader, Uriah Stephens, was a Freemason, Odd Fellow, and Knight of Pythias. The title Stephens was given, "Grand Master Workman," was already in use by the Masonic Knights of Malta. Over the next twenty years, the Knights of Labor would reach a membership as high as 2.5 million, or one in five American workers. In 1886, they led nearly 9,000 strikes against prominent capitalists, including the aforementioned Jay Gould and other important figures of industry.

By 1886, the Knights were being led by Terence Powderley, who ushered the organization into a period of openness with the public not previously known. He was inspired largely by his Roman Catholicism, which prevented him from joining most secret societies, though he was a member of the church-sanctioned Ancient Order of Hibernians. That same year, beginning with May Day demonstrations for an eight-hour workday in Chicago's Haymarket Square, strike demonstrations escalated into violent clashes with the police, taking the lives of four strikers at the McCormick plant. A pipe bomb was thrown when more police arrived on the scene. Eight conspirators, two of them Knights of Labor, stood trial for the bombing, with one committing suicide in his cell and four eventually convicted of murder and hanged in 1890. Powderley's refusal to speak up in support of the men, most significantly high-ranking Knight Albert Parsons, was the beginning of factional fighting within the Knights of Labor that eventually brought it down. Ironically, after Powderley's exit from the Knights, he joined the Catholic Church's Knights of Columbus, only to find it also was a secret society. He eventually left the Catholic Church and died a 33rd-degree Freemason (Weir 66).

The use of medieval trappings by the Knights of Labor indicates just how pervasive the late-nineteenth-century trend of medievalism had become. Some explanation for the term is perhaps required. English art critic John Ruskin coined the term "medievalism" in 1853 for application to a certain form of architecture, but it soon was applied to all areas of the arts and humanities. In the field of literature, one major event in the medievalist revival was the publication of several editions of Malory's *Morte d'Arthur* in Britain for the first time in nearly 200 years, including an 1817 edition compiled by then poet laureate Robert Southey. The subsequent forays into Arthuriana by Scott and Tennyson rekindled an interest in chivalry and courtly love that, as discussed above, "hopped the pond" and found fertile ground in the American South.

The medievalism that the Knights of Labor practiced is primarily evident in its embrace of elements of Freemasonry, which has its own legendary ties to medieval orders such as the Knights Templar, and which experienced a re-flowering in both England and America with the medievalist revival. Young Samuel Langhorne Clemens was among the many American men who flocked to Masonic halls as members in the mid-nineteenth century; he left after achieving his third Masonic degree (Hoffman 107). Robert Weir links the phenomenon of Freemasonry with the popularity of arcane ritual in the Knights of Labor:

> Ritual defined 'Knighthood' as an exalted model of personal behavior that dictated how members related to each other, and how they encountered the outside world. Put directly, ritual behavior was important to Gilded Age workers, fraternal experience bonded diffuse interests, and its mysteries had profound meaning for those who practiced it [*Beyond Labor's Veil* 21].

The Knights even maintained a Committee on Ritual, which issued reports at the Knights' meetings and conventions.

Medievalism also influenced the Knights in the form of folk history. One contemporaneous work on the Knights, W.K. Tisdale's *The Knights' Book*, published in 1886, claimed to trace the ancestry of the Knights of Labor all the way back to the early French ruler Hugh Capet in A.D. 998. The text on the title page read, "The Knights' Book — Matters Concerning Capital — The Principles and Aims of the Knights of Labor — Chivalry and Knighthood of the Middle Ages— The Passage of Arms— The Battle for Honor and Renown" (Weir 31-32). As far as their conduct was concerned, historian Robert Weir describes the "Ideal Knight" as "chaste, chivalrous, honest, patriotic, religious, temperate, and loyal to labor's cause" (*Beyond* 63). In fact, the Knights' position on temperance was strong enough for workers in the liquor industry to be banned from the organization outright. At one point in the Knights' history, even profanity was forbidden. Embracing chivalry, the Knights were no different from a large segment of American citizenry of the time, many of whom had joined fraternal organizations in imitation of the long-standing chivalric traditions of western Europe. Weir writes, "Medievalism and antimodernism held powerful sway in America, particularly among those most suspicious of emergent industrial society" (*Beyond* 25). The most suspicious would have been the workers, as they would be the easiest to exploit, so it is not surprising that, as Weir notes, the Knights were criticized for their connection to medievalism by more radical elements of the labor movement, who saw the chivalrous affectations as bourgeois "contamination" (*Beyond* 121).

Beyond the connections to Freemasonry, the Knights' medievalism is apparent in their publications. For instance, an explanation of the Knights' goals in an 1887 magazine article uses a distinctly medievalist metaphor:

> The proposition to persuade employers to arbitrate all differences that may arise between them and their employes [*sic*], in order that the bonds of sympathy between them may be strengthened, and that strikes may be rendered unnecessary, while holding out with one hand the calumet, points with the other to the sword [Scott "Mission" 478].

Besides news articles, many labor publications of the period included poems, songs, and fiction as well. This attention to reading material was intended to reflect the model of how a Knight would spend his leisure time. The concept of leisure is integral to the labor movement of the late nineteenth century, as a reduction in the working hours per day would leave several hours to do what one wished. Indicative of the style of this literature is "All Hail Labor Knights!!!" by Bulah Brinton, which typifies the spirit of courtly love that informs much of this poetry: "Fair ladies of honor come crown these brave Knights / God help them to gain men and women their just rights" (Weir 177-78).

The printing of poetry is a surprisingly good gauge of the Haymarket riots' effect on the culture of the Knights. In 1885 and 1886, the *Journal of United Labor* (*JUL*) published some thirty poems per year; in 1887, they published 148 poems. Further, Weir notes that "before 1886, the *JUL* favored classic poems from Tennyson, Scott, and Pope.... By 1887, the *JUL* printed poems from more vociferous poets.... By 1892, the *JUL* had changed so much that the socialist paper *The Weekly People* urged its readership to read it" (*Beyond* 172).

The post-Haymarket poetry can largely be divided into pro- and anti-Powderley points of view. For instance, a Knights publication called *John Swinton's Paper* published, in early 1887, "K. of L., A Poem of Sir Powderley." Weir writes that in the poem Powderley "appears as a medieval knight-errant leading the KOL on a holy crusade to bring the working and employing classes together. In his quest, Powderley is tasked by scabs, Pinkertons, and skeptics" (*Beyond* 176). An 1890 ode to Powderley in the *Journal of the Knights of Labor* reads, in part: "Though no helmet his brow is adorning / As his cavalry sweeps o'er the plains, / There is manhood outraged in his scorning, / And the blood of a king in his veins" (Weir 177). Notably, echoing the observation that the more radical labor factions saw the medievalist fad as bourgeois, anti-Powderley poetry either mocked the chivalrous mood of the pro-Powderley poetry and the Knights in general or avoided the trappings altogether.

Notable among the fiction of the Knights of Labor publications is a serialized novel called *The Orphan Sisters: Daughters of the Knights of Labor*. The novel details the relationship between Knight of Labor Mark Talford and Lillian Marchmont. Lillian is stabbed by Olga, daughter of factory owner (and villain) Magnus Hartwell, who then purchases a "Nubian drug" from Judith Bunch to make Mark her "love slave." Lillian turns up alive after all, and Olga's plan is foiled. The story bears some resemblance to the Tristan and Isolde myth incorporated into Malory's *Morte* and that reappeared in Arnold's poetry. While Arnold's "Civilisation in the United States" was one major salvo in a war of cultures that found expression in *Connecticut Yankee*, Hank Morgan's destruction of Camelot at the Battle of the Sand Belt can be read as yet another attack on the British monarchy via their national mythology. However, there is much to suggest that the culture of the Knights of Labor played a pivotal role in Twain's ending too.

In March 1886, when Twain had just begun writing *Connecticut Yankee*, he addressed the Monday Evening Club in Hartford with a speech on the topic of the threatening rise of the Knights of Labor. This was a particularly prescient choice of subject matter, as the name of the Knights would be on the lips of many Americans because of Haymarket just two months later. The subject was on Twain's mind because he had encountered a very prominent Knight, James Welsh, in January 1886 at the U.S. Senate Committee on Patents, where Welsh spoke against certain copyright legislation that Twain, along with the poet James Russell

Lowell, was there to support. Twain's speech contained the following lines:

> [A king] will win the grateful tears of a multitude of slaves by setting them free ... and then laugh in their faces and tear up their emancipation papers, and promise them a bitterer and crueler slavery than they ever imagined.... [G]ive it to the noblesse of the Middle Ages, and they will claim and seize wandering freedmen as their serfs.... [G]ive it to the Church, and she will burn, flay, slay torture, massacre, ruthlessly ... ["Dynasty" 883].

Here Twain has touched on nearly every key issue that would eventually appear in *Connecticut Yankee*.

Welsh had spoken before Congress so eloquently that Twain switched points of view on the copyright issue. Smith and Gibson write, "[Twain] might well have been further impressed by the debating skill Welsh showed in an interchange with [Lowell] before the Committee" (Twain and Howells 598). Summing up his influence on Twain, Smith and Gibson write that Welsh was "in one sense the prototype of Hank Morgan in *A Connecticut Yankee*" (Twain and Howells 598). Philip Foner posits that the Hartford speech became "the basis of his discussion of trade unionism and trade-union haters in Chapter XXXIII of [*Connecticut Yankee*]," the aforementioned chapter on "Sixth Century Political Economy" (*Social Critic* 175-76). Smith offers as evidence of his claim the fact that Chapter XXXIII was read for many years at labor union meetings. This evidence is corroborated by the fact that protection was a major issue for the Knights and that they opposed setting wages in favor of competition.

The Knights of Labor were still on Twain's mind as he forwarded a copy of the speech in a letter to Howells in March 1888. Haymarket had further oriented Twain, and especially Howells, toward the Knights. Howells had written a letter to the *New York Tribune* in November 1886 in defense of the so-called Haymarket anarchists and continued to write to Twain over the next several years on issues concerning the Knights and labor in general (Twain and Howells *passim*). In the first six months after Haymarket, Twain found himself finishing the first three chapters of *A Connecticut Yankee*, only to put the manuscript aside for nearly a year. In November 1886, Twain read the first three chapters to a military association assembly in New York, and he gave a synopsis of how he planned to end the book. Already, that ending was going to be vio-

lent. In this early version, Arthur first commissions Hank Morgan to kill
the rival kings of England. Twain continues: "Having done this, knocked
the ogres out of commission, and abolished courtly love and armour,
the Yankee puts the kingdom on a strictly business basis. Arthur's
knights set themselves up as a stock exchange and the going rate for a
seat at the Round Table reaches thirty thousand dollars" (Kaplan 18).

Twain assured his audience then that he intended not to disgrace
the most famous of Malory's characters, such as Launcelot and Merlin.
Still, Hank's resolution to "abolish courtly love" speaks directly to the
issue of attacking medievalism and its perceived ill effects. Later, Twain
would change his mind and render Arthur, Launcelot, and others as
buffoons and would destroy them all. Significantly, even at this early
date in the novel's composition, Twain biographer Andrew Hoffman's
analysis is correct: "What had begun as a comic fancy, with the vision
of a modern man desperately uncomfortable in a suit of armor, had
developed into a seriocomic contrast between democratic and hierar-
chic political systems" (*Inventing Mark Twain* 340). If, as Leslie
Workman has said, medievalism can be defined as "the continuing
process of creating the Middle Ages [Verduin]," then what we are presented with in *Connecticut Yankee* is anti-medievalism in that we are
shown the *destruction* of the Middle Ages.

After Haymarket, when he worked on the *Connecticut Yankee* manuscript again in the summers of 1887 and 1888, and then in the winter
of 1889, when he finished the novel, Twain was unable to wrest humor
out of the Yankee's situation without some violent event happening as
well. Hoffman writes, "Whenever he started the book of in a new direction, his Yankee ran into some arbitrary malicious authority" (*Inventing*
345). Hoffman characterizes the ideological struggle behind the death
throes of Camelot:

> [Twain's] mix of radical political ideology and pessimistic
> determinism drove the book's hero, Hank Morgan, into
> impossible compromises. Hank's democratic reform of civi-
> lization combated his misanthropic drive to rule it all. Hank,
> like Sam, wanted to dominate his world through public accla-
> mation of his technological superiority. Both wanted to leave
> the decision to the people, but neither would accept that there
> was equal justice inherent in the possibility that his own ideas
> might suffer defeat [*Inventing* 354-55].

Twain may also be making a veiled reference to Terence Powderley with

Connecticut Yankee's violent ending. Although Smith's point concerning the possible influence of Welsh on the character of Hank Morgan is relevant, Morgan's characterization is also informed by Twain himself. After all, this is a *Connecticut* Yankee, and Twain spent the last several decades of his life in Hartford. Further, Smith also suggests that Haymarket's affects on Twain found their way into the character of Hank. Smith writes, "[Hank's] reaction to the fear-inspired, retaliatory mob hangings ... in 'The Tragedy of the Manor House' in the *Connecticut Yankee* (Chapter XXX), suggest that Clemens may have shared Howells's indignation if not his surprise over the condemnation and execution of four of the eight defendants in a mood of national hysteria" (Twain & Howells 581). It should be borne in mind that Powderley did nothing to mitigate the circumstances for the two Knights who stood trial and were executed for Haymarket and that this inaction was seen as a betrayal. Predicting, perhaps, that the Knights would not survive the rift over Haymarket, Twain symbolized the union's ultimate demise through the complete destruction of Camelot.

The influence of *A Connecticut Yankee in King Arthur's Court* on later Arthurian works by American writers cannot be overestimated. Mark Twain's establishment of an Arthurian voice distinct from the English prototype in its American sensibilities found echoes in the works of Raymond Chandler and Bernard Malamud. The lampooning of medievalism in the novel was reiterated by James Branch Cabell. The North-South dichotomy that Twain tapped was further explored by Stark Young and Walker Percy. And the association of the Arthurian myth with contemporary politics found fertile ground in the works of John Steinbeck and Donald Barthelme. Twain's American predecessors, Emerson and Hawthorne among them, began the process, but it was Twain who opened the gates and officially ushered Arthurian literature into America.

CHAPTER II

Steinbeck's Early Novels

There are few writers of any nationality whose work has been more informed by the Arthurian legends than that of John Steinbeck. From his first novel, *Cup of Gold*, to the rendering of Malory's *Morte d'Arthur* into modern English that he left unfinished when he died, Steinbeck relied on Camelot for his inspiration even more than on the Bible or Classical mythology — favorites for contemporaries like Faulkner, Eliot, and O'Neill. The novels that Steinbeck wrote before his journalistic and government-commissioned work during World War II share a strong idealization of chivalry as presented in Malory, along with a realization, often poignant, that this ideal was no longer attainable. This epiphany finds expression specifically in Steinbeck's depiction of the Grail quest, which crops up in venues as varied as colonial Panama, the Monterey, California, of Steinbeck's youth, and California's orchards during a period of labor unrest.

Steinbeck grew up in the first decade of the twentieth century, and he was among the first generation of American children immersed in the Arthurian legend from childhood. Writers and illustrators such as Howard Pyle, Andrew Lang, and William Henry Frost consistently shaped the myth into a decidedly American incarnation, wherein individualism and status achieved through hard work were stressed above the idea of noble birth and the divine right of kings. Beginning with Sidney Lanier's volume of Arthuriana for children, *The Boy's King Arthur* (1880), American audiences were increasingly exposed to the Camelot myth. Lanier was precisely the sort of writer that Twain sought to attack in *Connecticut Yankee*. The author was a Southerner, and *The Boy's King Arthur* was a seminal text in the American medievalist revival, extolling the chivalric values that Twain disdained to American children from the earliest age. Jeanne Fox-Friedman notes that the introduction to

another of Lanier's boys' books makes an explicit reference to the application of chivalric myth to day-to-day conduct ("Chivalric Order" 148):
"As you read of the fair knights ... it cannot but occur to you that somehow it seems harder to be a good knight nowadays than it was then....
Nevertheless the same qualities which made a manful fighter then make
one now" (Lanier *Froissart* viii-x).

When, as noted in Chapter 1, William Byron Forbush established
the Knights of King Arthur, a scouting group based on the English model
of Baden-Powell, the guidelines stressed an American ideal:

> [T]he most cogent reason yet given for the roundness of the
> table is that at a round table there is no head, and so there
> can be no jealousy. Thus we have, in a democracy under lead-
> ership, the ideal form of organization of boys [Lupack
> "Figure" 127; Forbush 29].

While there is no evidence that Steinbeck was part of such a group
as a child, he was apparently introduced to the Arthurian myth at a very
early age: his Aunt Molly gave him Malory's *Morte* when he was nine
(Parini *Steinbeck* 14). (There are some who believe that Steinbeck's first
exposure to Malory was actually none other than Lanier's *Boy's King
Arthur* [Prindle 25].) Soon the young Steinbeck was telling medieval-
styled stories to his sister Mary, who grew to share his love of the
Arthurian myth. In the last years before he died, Steinbeck intended to
dedicate his modern English rendering of Malory to Mary:

> It sometimes happens in sadness and pity that faithful ser-
> vice is not appreciated, so my fair and loyal sister remained
> unrecognized as squire — Wherefore this day I make amends
> within my power and raise her to knighthood and give her
> praise.— And from this hour she shall be called Sir Marie
> Steinbeck of Salinas Valley.— God give her worship without
> peril [*Acts* vi].

Having grown up in such an environment and at a time when Americans
were promoting a version of the Arthurian legend in which the "king"
was one of the people, Steinbeck's use of the myth in his early works
reflects this delicate tension between individualism and the greatest good
for the greatest number. When Steinbeck veers toward individualism in
his characterizations, achievement comes hand-in-hand with villainy.
When the needs of the group take precedence, the entire enterprise is
ultimately doomed.

Cup of Gold (1929), Steinbeck's first novel, demonstrated weaknesses in Steinbeck's style that he would eventually overcome. The story tracks privateer Henry Morgan's life from his adolescence in Wales to his plundering of Panama City, which the pirates dubbed the "Cup of Gold," and his later knighting by the British monarchy for his efforts. It bears mentioning that Steinbeck chose the seventeenth century, i.e., a very early part of the modern era, as the period on which to impose the instabilities of medievalism. The implication is that any application of medieval myth outside its own period — even as chronologically close as the seventeenth century — is inherently problematic. The novel's central, medieval metaphor is one of the most literal in Steinbeck's canon, and this heavy-handedness is apparent in the work, as when Morgan tells his lieutenant, Coeur de Gris, "Now we will take the Cup of Gold together, and it shall be a chalice of two handles" (*Cup of Gold* 151). Steinbeck has the cup serve a dual purpose: It is an epithet for Panama City and the figurative Grail that will restore Morgan and de Gris.

Shortly after conquering Panama, Morgan meets La Santa Roja, the woman named Ysobel of whom he has heard in pirates' legends and whom he has highly idealized in his own mind, but who falls short of his fantasized expectations. We should note here the similarity of the name to the mythical Yseult (a variant of Isolde) of the Arthurian cycle, who is pursued by Tristan but remains unattainable. Thus, like the cup itself, she stands as a symbol of intangible ideals. Immediately following Morgan's first encounter with La Santa Roja comes one of the most remarkable passages in the novel, as Morgan is looking over his booty from the plunder of Panama:

> Henry Morgan lifted a golden cup from the heap of loot. It was a lovely, slender chalice with long curved handles and a rim of silver. Around its outer edge four grotesque lambs chased each other, and inside, on the bottom, a naked girl lifted her arms in sensual ecstasy. The captain turned the cup in his hands. Then, suddenly, he hurled it at a little fiery pyramid of diamonds [*Cup of Gold* 175].

Here we see the juxtaposition of the Grail that is Panama, the idealized, Grail-like woman, and an actual, *literal* Grail; and the emotion all this evokes from Morgan is frustration and disgust. The disillusionment of the Grail knight is plain.

As we have already noted, Steinbeck used the Grail quest as the principal Arthurian device in his early novels. Generally speaking, his use of the myth consists of progressively more abstract depictions of a Grail that is increasingly elusive in each work. Warren French has linked Steinbeck's use of the Grail legend to the poetry of T.S. Eliot and Edwin Arlington Robinson, the latter of whose trilogy of Arthurian-themed poems—"Merlin," "Lancelot," and "Tristram"—helped usher in a second Arthurian revival in the United States in the 1920s (French "Steinbeck's Use of Mallory" 4). Steinbeck had been rather explicit about what he intended the Grail quest to signify, writing once in a letter, "One who doubts that the trappings of the Grail quest are consistent with hooliganism need only observe the growing confusion of lawmen and outlaws in the legends of our own West" (French *John Steinbeck* 60). Steinbeck was drawing an analogy between the white-hatted gunslinger of the "Wild West" tradition and the knight errant of medieval myth and legend. Furthermore, Steinbeck expressed the belief that street gangs in the 1950s and 1960s could be seen as yet another version of the need to impose a code of conduct on a chaotic environment.

Morgan is dealing with the same sort of difficulty in *Cup of Gold*. As French has noted, this novel is one in which "Grail-questers learn they must split up or go under" (French "Steinbeck's" 5). The tension between the desires of the individual and the needs of the group is evident even at this early date.

Steinbeck's ambivalence toward the Grail quest in *Cup of Gold* also has some basis in the history of his subject matter. Panama was the setting of one of the first instances of American imperialism, with Theodore Roosevelt's Panama Canal project strongly underscoring the Monroe Doctrine of U.S. hegemony in the Western Hemisphere. At the time of its opening in 1914, the Canal was the crowning achievement in a century ushered in by the establishment of American military supremacy from San Juan Hill to the Philippines via the Spanish-American war—during which Roosevelt established himself as a national hero. Fox-Friedman links Roosevelt directly to the Arthurian myth, calling him the "ideal figure of [our] crusading imperialism" and the "modern embodiment of the chivalric knight" ("Order" 152), and citing a letter sent to Roosevelt by a Wyoming resident that dubbed him "a modern Sir Galahad" ("Order" 153). The reference to the Grail quest here is in the figure of Galahad, the knight who achieves the Grail in Malory.

Returning to Steinbeck's text, Henry Morgan serves as a particularly apt stand-in for American imperialism, since, like Roosevelt, he achieves greatness by defeating the Spanish. But Morgan's own feeling about such imperialism is far from Roosevelt's secure "big stick" attitude. Morgan's eventual marriage to a British debutante and acquisition of the office of the Governor-General of Jamaica imply his capitulation to the established society he had initially rebelled against. The lines get blurry here: Britain has traditionally been associated with the chivalric tradition; therefore by accepting a position in this government, it would seem Morgan has embraced the tradition fully. Yet Morgan's disappointment at having achieved his highly romantic goals speaks to a less than complete acceptance of the tradition. What this ambivalence may suggest instead is Morgan's realization — mirroring Steinbeck's own philosophical position — that rugged individualism must ultimately temper itself according to the dictates of the greater community, which in this case is the British Empire. We can associate the individualistic aspect of Morgan's nature with Roosevelt and his form of Americanism that would dictate the ideals of personal achievement and anti-collectivist economics to the rest of the world. Later in his career, particularly during and after World War II, Steinbeck's point of view concerning America's role in the world would change, and this shift in perspective would find similar expression in his works.

Steinbeck's prominent use of Arthurian symbolism in *Cup of Gold* extends to the characters, particularly their names. It is worth noting that, despite it being more a question of historical accuracy than conscious choice, Steinbeck's protagonist has the same name as Twain's Connecticut Yankee. This parallelism might suggest areas of intersection between the two texts, but there are relatively few. Both Captain Morgan and Hank are iconoclastic knights who find functioning within the prescribed chivalric tradition difficult if not impossible. For the Yankee, this disability is a function of his predisposition against medieval chivalry; for Captain Morgan, disaffection comes from disillusionment when he realizes that the reality of the world is far different from the tradition he learned in his youth. Twain's Morgan alters his reality to fit his point of view, while Steinbeck's Morgan has his point of view shaped by reality.

Both authors are addressing the incongruity between medievalism and modernity, though they approach it from different angles. Steinbeck's association of the Morgan name with medievalism is apparent not only in *Cup of Gold*, but also in his subsequent story-cycle, *The Pastures of Heaven*. In that work, Molly Morgan appears as an auxiliary character in the context of the principal plot concerning the "cursed" Munroe family. Molly is a school teacher who reads to her students the poetry of Sir Walter Scott, among other Romantic works.

The difference in the ways Twain and Steinbeck approach medievalism finds some expression in Philip Rahv's landmark essay "Paleface and Redskin," in which the "dichotomy between experience and consciousness" (*Image and Idea* 1) is at the root of a rift in our national literature. Twain identified strongly with the redskin, or experience-oriented, side of the dichotomy; thus his disdain of Scott and Americans who emulated him, notably James Fenimore Cooper. Steinbeck, however, essentially straddled the paleface-redskin divide in *Cup of Gold*. On the one hand, Morgan's rugged individualism is emblematic of the Redskin tradition. On the other hand, his eventual assimilation into the English upper class implies Paleface tendencies. Dennis Prindle writes, "[N]arrative form in Steinbeck's novels is tied to some of the most basic myths informing the dream of culture in the west, or what in America Rahv characterized as the paleface hankering after religious norms and spiritual value" ("Pretexts" 24). In Steinbeck's subsequent pre-war works, the dichotomy is considerably less pronounced, as is the symbolism Steinbeck uses to depict the rift. As Prindle concludes, "For taking shape within *Cup of Gold* are the beginnings of what will be an enduring conflict in Steinbeck between tradition and experience, framed here with Arthurian romance on one side and a slyly ironic naturalism on the other" ("Pretexts" 27).

We should also consider the characterization of Merlin in each work. Arthurian scholar Alan Lupack has noted that Merlin appears frequently in works by American writers, and "his power to shape and control his environment brings him in line with recurring figures in American popular culture, such as Paul Bunyan or Superman" ("Figure" 121). This American literary tradition probably has its roots in the Merlin poetry of Ralph Waldo Emerson, in which Merlin is a bard whose poetry emanates from him in the way that an Aeolian harp issues music: "Merlin's blows are strokes of fate, / Chiming with the forest tone, / When boughs buffet boughs in the wood ..." ("Merlin" 448). Emerson also evokes the Merlin of Malory's *Morte*, in his essay "Poetry and Imagination," as an example of the "metallic force of primitive words [that] makes the superiority of the remains of the rude ages" ("Poetry" 58).

Both Twain's and Steinbeck's uses of Merlin diverge from the Emersonian prototype, however. As we have seen in Chapter I, Merlin appears in *Connecticut Yankee* as the archenemy whom Hank can defeat only by using the superior magic of technology. In *Cup of Gold*, Merlin appears in a quite different form. Steinbeck's unusual characterization presents Merlin as a sort of Welsh magus—a wise man of Morgan's town who gives advice to the young pirate and who tries unsuccessfully to impress upon him the ultimate futility of attempting to achieve his goals. Merlin is therefore a far less radical character in Steinbeck than in Twain. He symbolizes a very anti-individualist, establishment-oriented point of view, though this opinion has presumably come through experience, as Morgan's eventually will as well. In this sense, Steinbeck's characterization of Merlin is closer to Malory's, in which the magician is, as Lupack describes him, a "tool of fate" ("Figure" 123), though we should note that Lupack's concept of fate here is more indicative of determinism than of the naturalistic fate that Emerson evokes in the lines from his poem "Merlin" quoted above.

Prindle offers an interesting parallel between the figure of Merlin in *Cup of Gold* and Steinbeck's youthful exposure to Sidney Lanier. He notes that Lanier's introduction to *The Boy's King Arthur* was "a rather apologetic summons to romance and the ideal of chivalry in a scientific age" ("Pretexts" 26). Then, noting the tendency of Steinbeck's Merlin toward conservatism and restraint, Prindle continues, "It is as though the old man [Merlin] were voicing that apologetic plea for chivalry and the often flawed idealism of romance from Lanier's introduction to *The Boy's King Arthur*." He concludes that, while "[o]utwardly the stuff of swashbuckling romance, Morgan's story is from first to last an empty and ironic re-enactment of a familiar narrative, Steinbeck's answer to those turn-of-the-century historical romances, with their dreaming heroes and high adventure" ("Pretexts" 29).

Steinbeck's reaction to myth here works on several levels. For instance, while he has idealized the chivalric ideal as presented in Lanier, his realization that the ideal is obsolete finds its expression through the same myth. So, relying on those very same characters—here, Merlin—who first expressed these ideals to make a point, Steinbeck uses them to make an entirely different point. Underlying the whole process in this case is perhaps the notion that the idea is inherently flawed from the beginning. If Prindle is correct in stating that Steinbeck's characterization of Merlin still relies on the chivalric tradition, then ultimately it is chivalry itself that is to blame, and not modernity or an innate human inability to always be noble.

Steinbeck biographer Jay Parini believes the characterization of Merlin in *Cup of Gold* owes much to James Branch Cabell (*Steinbeck* 81); in fact, Steinbeck acknowledged in a letter to A. Grove Day after the novel's publication (Steinbeck and Wallsten, 1975 17–18) that Cabell was indeed a great influence, not only on the character of Merlin, but also on the mock-romantic style of the novel as a whole. In Chapter XVIII of Cabell's *Jurgen*, the title character is summoned by Merlin Ambrosius after having rescued Guenevere from captivity in an underground chamber. Just as Merlin in *Cup of Gold* warns young Morgan that he is likely to be disappointed by chasing his fantasies, the Merlin of *Jurgen* discourages the pawnbroker from accompanying the Round Table to London, saying, "I warn you that for you to come with us to London would not be convenient" (*Jurgen* 114). There is of course a difference between the two situations, in that while Steinbeck's Merlin wishes only to have Morgan avoid disillusionment, Cabell's Merlin is interceding to prevent Jurgen from stealing Guenevere from Arthur, her betrothed. However, if we consider that an important metaphor for Morgan's disappointment is La Santa Roja, another analogue between *Cup of Gold* and the Merlin story arises. In Malory, Merlin's power is robbed from him by Nimue, the so-called Lady of the Lake, who casts a spell on him that imprisons him for eternity in the trunk of a tree; La Santa Roja has a similar effect on Morgan, having enchanted him, albeit in a less "magical" manner. Thus Cabell's Merlin is not only a source for Steinbeck's wizard but for the young pirate as well. Our clue that such a relationship is at work is found in *Jurgen*, when Merlin states that the issue of Jurgen's dalliance with Guenevere was brought to his attention by Dame Anaitis (113), whose name is one of several for the Lady of the Lake in the various Arthurian legends.

Steinbeck followed up *Cup of Gold* with *Pastures of Heaven* in 1932. While *Pastures* featured a character with an Arthurian name — Molly Morgan — *To a God Unknown*, the next novel, was virtually devoid of Arthurian references and relied instead on the Hebrew Bible. In *Tortilla Flat* (1935), however, Steinbeck returned to the Arthurian schema, producing the most Malory-influenced work of his canon with the exception of his unfinished modern English rendering of the *Morte*.

Tortilla Flat sets *Le Morte d'Arthur* in Monterey, California, among the so-called *paisanos* of the area, who are "led" by Danny, the only property owner among them. Steinbeck wrote in the preface to the novel of the house of Danny, the novel's Arthur figure, that it "was not unlike the Round Table, and Danny's friends were not unlike the Knights of it" (*Tortilla Flat* 373). Further, Steinbeck titled each chapter in the fashion of the Caxton manuscript of Malory; for instance, "How Danny brooded and became mad. How the devil in the shape of Torelli assaulted Danny's House."

We should note that Steinbeck only added the Caxton-style chapter titles, along with the prefatory remarks concerning Danny's house as a Round Table symbol, once he was finished the first draft of the novel and his readers were having difficulty finding the Arthurian material embedded in the text (Fontenrose "*Tortilla*" 24-25). Lupack notes that the links between Steinbeck's and Malory's characters might have been difficult to distinguish because the dramatis personae of *Tortilla Flat* are "in many ways just the opposite of an idealized view of Arthur and the knights of the Round Table.... They are, in fact, common men, in some ways the most common of men" (Lupack "Figure" 133-34). In Lupack's point of view, the general savaging of the myth through the debasement of the principal characters of the myth — Arthur, Launcelot, Galahad, and Percival — is fundamental to Steinbeck's project.

The converse of this argument is that Steinbeck seeks to invest in these common men all the dignity of a medieval monarch and court, and Lupack recognizes this possibility, writing that Steinbeck "like other American authors before him sees the possibility that any person can be Arthur" ("Figure" 135). Perhaps, then, what lies at the bottom of the use of the Arthurian myth by American writers — something that Steinbeck may have been the first such author to recognize — is both sides of this argument working simultaneously. While the American tradition of democracy dictates that any American should and could be as noble as the next, it is impossible not to upset the delicate nature of the Arthurian myth by giving it such an egalitarian gloss. This is perhaps why, as we have begun to see, the Grail quests of Steinbeck's early novels had to fail — because they were flawed in their basic intent.

French is careful to note that there is more than one Grail quest in *Tortilla Flat* (Steinbeck 54-55), though the most prominent example is in Chapter VIII — "How Danny's Friends sought mystic treasure on St. Andrew's Eve. How Pilon found it and later how a pair of serge pants changed ownership twice." Examining elements of the chapter and finding where they resonate in the medieval form of the Grail myth reveals Steinbeck's continued depiction of the Grail as an unattainable ideal. At the same time, this novel's strong debasement of elements of the myth suggests that not only is the Grail beyond reach, but so also is the conduct becoming of a knight who would undertake such a task. For instance, the chapter title, particularly its mention of the serge pants, has a strong association with the Grail quest in *Le Morte d'Arthur*. Malory placed the Grail quest in Books XIII and XIV of the *Morte* (according to the divisions of the Caxton manuscript, whose chapter style Steinbeck mimicked in *Tortilla Flat*), and in Chapter 4 of Book XIII, the chapter heading in Malory is "How the old man brought Galahad to the Siege Perilous and set him therein, and how all the knights marvelled." In this chapter, Galahad's identity as the knight who will find the Holy Grail is revealed to the Round Table. Our clue that the "serge pants" of Steinbeck's work have their origins in the Siege Perilous is the initial letters of the words in question.

In *Tortilla Flat*, the serge pants of Chapter VIII are stolen from Big Joe Portagee by Pilon, the "knight" of Danny's retinue who finds the "Grail," as punishment for Big Joe's having stolen from Danny. Pilon trades the stolen pants to Torelli's wife for a bottle of wine, but when he is short-changed he steals them back and returns them to Joe, telling him Torelli's wife had stolen them in the first place. Thus, not only is the Siege Perilous recast in mundane terms as a pair of pants, but the Grail knight is also similarly debased, as he is depicted as a thief and a liar.

Steinbeck's decision to portray the Siege Perilous as a stolen pair of pants may also have its basis in Malory. The first chapter of Malory's Book XV tells of "How Sir Launcelot came into a chapel, where he found dead, in a white shirt, a man of religion, of an hundred winter old" (Malory 291). In this episode, Launcelot, while himself on the Grail quest, debates with an old man whether or not the white shirt of a particular knightly order should still be worn by a dead man. Launcelot argues unsuccessfully that the corpse should be stripped of the garment, but the old man tells the knight he is wrong. The association between the serge pants and the white shirt is tenuous, but it can serve as another example of how Steinbeck profanes the Grail myth, since while Launcelot does not defile the dead body by taking its shirt, Pilon steals the serge pants without any moral qualms.

While in Malory the Grail quest begins on the Christian holiday of Pentecost, fifty days after Easter and the day on which the apostles were conferred with the Holy Spirit, Steinbeck has his principal Grail quest begin on St. Andrew's Eve, November 29. The reasons for this shift in dates are unclear, though Steinbeck gives one explanation in the thoughts of Joe Portagee:

> Then the Portagee knew; for this was the night when every paisano who wasn't in jail wandered restlessly through the forest. This was the night when all buried treasure sent up a faint phosphorescent glow through the ground. There was plenty of treasure in the woods, too. Monterey had been invaded many times in two hundred years, and each time valuables had been hidden in the earth [*Tortilla Flat* 432].

So it seems that St. Andrew's Eve holds this significance for Monterey, though no larger reason for the date is given.

Some consideration of the significance of St. Andrew and his feast day for Christians sheds additional light on the situation. However, it is important to note that St. Andrew's Eve is traditionally associated with Advent, the four weeks preceding Christmas. So on one level, Steinbeck may be drawing a parallel between Jesus and Danny, and in this sense, he is continuing Malory's identification of Arthur with Jesus. In the finale of *Le Morte*, Arthur is in Avalon and there is every expectation that he will return, in the same way that Jesus ascends into Heaven at the close of the Gospels, and the apostles are given to understand that he will return some day.

On the other hand, there is no expectation that Danny will return after death. In fact, Steinbeck is careful to note that unlike Jesus, who rises from the dead after two* days, Danny instead is *given* his funeral mass and burial, and the narrator notes, "Danny was dead, two days dead; and already he had ceased to be Danny" (*Tortilla Flat* 521). Thus the desire on Steinbeck's part to move the date of the Grail quest away from Pentecost may indicate an intention to dissociate the quest from one episode of the return of Jesus, here in the form of the Holy Spirit. As if to underscore the point, Danny's friends destroy his one surviving house and burn it to the ground, as they had already done to Danny's other house. Another possible significance of Steinbeck's choice of St. Andrew's Eve as the date of the Grail quest is Andrew the apostle's role as a "fisher of men" for Jesus. Andrew, with his brother, Peter, helped to gather a wide ring of disciples around their messiah. If we consider this model with Danny's identification as a Christ figure in mind, we can see a similar congregation building around Danny when his friends move into his house.

Still, John Timmerman points out that despite the novel's sad end-

Christian tradition refers to the time period as three days, but Jesus is dead only from Friday afternoon to Sunday morning.

ing, *Tortilla Flat* owes a much greater debt to the genre of tragicomedy than to tragedy. Setting forth genre definitions similar to those in Northrop Frye's *Anatomy of Criticism*, Timmerman remarks that all of Steinbeck's so-called Cannery Row novels fit the tragicomic mode insofar as the characters are of common birth, the plot begins with tragedy but ends with resolution, and the style is mock-epic (Timmerman 140). Here we can see another profaning of the traditional Arthurian story cycle, with the high elements of tragedy as found in Malory being individually lowered. Whereas, using Timmerman's example, Shakespeare's Hamlet is a prince of noble birth in a play written in blank verse that ends tragically, Steinbeck's Danny is a peasant who speaks, at his most polished moments, in a broad burlesque of high medieval style. And, Timmerman concludes, though Danny's death could be construed as a tragic element, instead it is "attended by all the trappings of comedy" (154), and he cites the house-destroying wake held for Danny as proof.

Despite these differences, however, Joseph Fontenrose has written, "The structural plan of Malory's *Arthur* had to be condensed for use as a model for *Tortilla Flat*, and one rescue of a maid in distress will do for twenty. But Malory's Arthur story did in fact determine the narrative sequence and pervade the whole content" (*Tortilla* 25). Among the examples Fontenrose provides are the relationship of Steinbeck's Pirate to Pelles, the Maimed King in Malory who is the keeper of the Grail. At the same time, Fontenrose posits that Pirate is also Steinbeck's stand-in for Malory's Percival, in that Pirate stands somewhat outside Danny's inner circle, sleeping in a corner of Danny's house with his dogs, rather than with the rest of the "knights" in one of the rooms (26). While the ambiguity of the associations between Malory's and Steinbeck's casts of characters lends itself to confusion, Fontenrose offers a caveat that "we need not suppose that Danny is always Arthur, Pilon always Launcelot" (25). While such confusion in character roles arises from the source materials themselves (for example, in some versions of the Grail story, Percival is the knight who finds the Grail, while in others, notably Malory, the successful knight is Galahad), Steinbeck continues this confusion in an admittedly simpler text, thus suggesting a persistent, if not increased, pointlessness to such questing in the modern world. We should also note that Danny dies and his house is destroyed despite the Grail quest that his friends undertake, unlike the Fisher King, who is rejuvenated by the Grail once it is found. In this way, we can see the ultimate futility of the quest as Steinbeck sees it.

Pilon is the "knight" among Danny's friends who finally finds the "grail." Steinbeck's characterization of Pilon is notable in comparison to the traditionally pure Grail knight. We have already noted that, despite his ability to discover the grail, Pilon is still a drunkard and a thief. This criminality extends all the way to Danny himself. As French writes, Danny and his friends resemble Sir Thomas Malory more than the knights that Malory depicted: Malory was a convicted robber and rapist who, it is believed, composed his *Morte* while in jail (French *Steinbeck* 60). Danny and the other *paisanos* father children out of wedlock, drink to excess in nearly every scene of the novel, and frequently steal, even from one another. This broad condemnation of the character of these "knights" also echoes T.S. Eliot's depiction of the degeneracy of society in "The Waste Land." In the same way that Eliot attributed moral decay in part to the ravages of World War I by casting some of the personas of his poem as veterans, Steinbeck portrays Danny, Pilon, and Joe Portagee as veterans of the same conflict. In this way, not only is their own degeneracy in part attributable to their war experiences, but their relationship to Grail questing is given more weight by the additional intertextual association.

When, on St. Andrew's Eve, Pilon (here filling Galahad's role from Malory) finds the Grail, what he actually unearths is a U.S. Geodetic Survey marker put there just a few years before, in 1915. Pilon remarks immediately how unsuccessfully this Grail quest has ended: "'Johnny Pom-pom found one,' he said with a quietness of great disappointment. 'Johnny Pom-pom took the metal piece and tried to sell it. It is a year in jail to dig one of these up,' Pilon mourned. 'A year in jail and two thousand dollar fine'" (*Tortilla Flat* 440). When Pilon goes with Big Joe from the digging site to get drunk, the serge pants episode follows. French has suggested that what is truly symbolized in unearthing the survey marker is the ultimate encroachment of a Huck Finn-style "sivilization" upon the more pure (though less law-abiding) lifestyle of the *paisanos*. Again, the Grail quest, though nominally successful, has failed in its ultimate goal — the salvation of the knights and their king. They are also reminded of the government that had considered them good enough to be drafted during wartime, but not good enough to be allowed to live outside their own segregated communities. This is perhaps one reason that Steinbeck has Pilon and Joe Portagee — two of the only veterans in the group —find the Grail-symbol, rather than someone who had not been taken advantage of by the government in such a way. In these respects, Pilon greatly resembles the "knights" of *Cannery Row*, in particular Hazel (Timmerman 150), whom Steinbeck casts as his Grail knight in that work and its sequel, *Sweet Thursday* (see Chapter V).

Outside the central Grail quest in *Tortilla Flat*, there are several other ways in which the Arthurian legends manifest themselves in the work. For example, Prindle seizes on the "Talismanic Bond" that Steinbeck attributes to the *paisanos* and symbolizes rather overtly through Danny's property and houses, and he concludes that the bond refers to the knightly system of *comitatus*, in which one swears greater loyalty to one's king and fellow knights than to one's family (Prindle 33). Similarly, Danny's madness in Chapter XV, when he leaves the group and his houses and picks fights and commits robberies in the town, is perhaps symbolic of Merlin's madness in the Arthurian cycle, when the wizard departs from Camelot and wanders the moors during a heavy storm. Then, when Danny's companions go out searching for their leader, another sort of Grail quest is presented.

Even the novel's final chapter affords a sort of Grail quest, when Danny leaves his house to engage in final and fatal conflict the "Enemy who is worthy of Danny." We should note that the Grail quest in the Arthurian myth is often linked to the Knights of the Round Table not by the Fisher King myth of the wounded king, but rather out of apathy among the knights and a desire by Arthur to rekindle in his retinue the spirit of chivalry and courtly love. Timmerman offers a unique twist on this final Grail quest in *Tortilla Flat*, suggesting that Danny's final outing constitutes the hero "stalk[ing] out against his personal Mordred" (154). In the same way that, in Malory, Arthur is complicit in his own downfall by fathering Mordred in the first place, Danny is partly to blame for the "Enemy who is worthy" of him because of his innate inability to keep his mind sufficiently occupied and his body out of trouble. And in both cases, the interaction between each Arthur and his Mordred proves fatal, as Mordred slays Arthur in battle, and Danny falls to his death in a drainage ditch.

In the same way that *Cup of Gold*'s protagonist exemplified the tension in Steinbeck's early novels between individual achievement and the greater good of the whole group, each of the "knights" of *Tortilla Flat* typifies this strain. However, in Steinbeck's novel, it is not for individual achievement that the characters abandon the group, but rather for superficial and selfish reasons. Pilon's leasing of Danny's other house in Chapters II and III serves as an example of this process. While Danny has been generous in charging Pilon a reasonable rent, Pilon begins trouble by being delinquent with his payments. The end result of Danny and Pilon's conflict is the burning of the house Danny is renting to Pilon. In this way, Danny is essentially half-destroyed, with his complete destruction in death coinciding with the burning of his other house.

Conversely, it is through the burning of the rental house that Pilon and the other friends come to live together in the remaining house. It is also through this process that Danny's final descent begins. Thus we can see that the actions of the friends as individuals have an important effect on the group as a whole, and, furthermore, we can see that despite a seemingly greater cohesiveness of the group after individual dissent has ended, in truth the result is the weakening of the group as a whole.

The year after publishing *Tortilla Flat*, Steinbeck released *In Dubious Battle*. Using information culled from his coverage of strikes among California's migrant laborers during the Great Depression (published in *The Harvest Gypsies* and followed up in fictional form with *Of Mice and Men* and *The Grapes of Wrath*), Steinbeck produced an account of a strike among migrant fruit-pickers in the fictional Torgas Valley of California. The principal characters are Jim Nolan, the son of a murdered union worker, and Mac, a veteran organizer for the Communist party. The novel was widely read and equally widely criticized, with praise coming from Andre Gide and condemnation from Mary McCarthy, both of whom looked primarily at the sociological and political aspects of the novel. It earned Steinbeck a reputation as a left-leaning chronicler of labor.

As Helen Lojek has pointed out, Steinbeck's choice of name for his setting, Torgas, resembles an actual location, Tagus, a ranch near Tulare, California, where there was a strike among orchard workers in 1933 (Lojek 116). There may be a deeper significance to the decision to use the Tagus incident as the basis for the story. The name of the actual ranch comes from a river that flows through Spain and Portugal, known among Spaniards as the *Rio Teja*, which has two important historical associations. First, the Tagus was used as a water source for tempering swords, thus conveniently providing a medieval flavor by association. Second, the Tagus flows principally through the section of Spain known as La Mancha, where one of the most famous of medieval heroes, Miguel de Cervantes' Don Quixote, lived. By evoking Cervantes, Steinbeck recalls one of the earliest critiques of medieval values, casting his own efforts in doubt.

Parini casts the novel in a more Malory-oriented light, writing that Steinbeck's "early interest in Malory yielded a lifelong commitment to the notion of heroism and the nature of moral action and its effects upon a community" (*Steinbeck* 165). Early in the novel, Nolan recounts witnessing a strikebreaking and makes an Arthurian reference: "I climbed up on the pedestal of that statue of Senator Morgan so I could see better" (*In Dubious Battle* 537). Parini's reasoning is based largely on French, who is one of the few Steinbeck critics to consider *In Dubious Battle* a depiction of a sort of Grail quest. Much of French's own argument hinges on the characterization of the novel's protagonist, Jim Nolan, as a Grail knight. French writes, "[There is a] remarkable psychological similarity between Jim Nolan, the central character of the novel, and one of the principal characters of the Round Table, Perceval or Parsifal as he is best known" (*Steinbeck* 65). While Galahad is perhaps a better designation for the case here, since he is the most chaste knight who succeeds in the Grail quest in Malory, Steinbeck's principal source of knowledge of Arthurian legend, French offers also that, like Percival, Nolan comes from a family with a slain father, an overly morose mother, and a sister who has vanished (*Steinbeck* 63). Nonetheless, French is correct in his suggestion that in his abstinence from sex, alcohol, and tobacco and his seemingly pure devotion to his cause — the Communist party and the liberation of workers — Nolan strongly resembles traditional representations of the archetypal knight-errant.

Immediately, however, several serious discrepancies arise between the traditional Grail story and *In Dubious Battle*. For example, while Nolan's quest to help the working classes through his labor struggles can be likened to a Grail quest of a kind, he is killed at the end of the novel, and the struggle simply continues. Despite his mythologically appropriate constitution for Grail-questing, he is not, in the final analysis, successful. And even more so than in *Cup of Gold* or *Tortilla Flat*, the "Grail" of this novel is a vast abstraction. Whereas in the first novel Steinbeck offered some large clues to the resonance of the story within the Grail legend, and in the second novel the openly stated Arthurian motif sheds light on the author's motivations, *In Dubious Battles* offers no such pointers. This novel's "Grails," Communism and worker liberation, are loosely defined goals that ultimately are better measured through progress than final results.

A major contributor to the problem here is the relationship between the Communist goal and the fundamental tension in Steinbeck's work, as we've already seen, between the group and the individual. *In Dubious Battle* is the first of Steinbeck's novels where he explored what he would eventually call the "group-man" concept, the biological construct whereby an organism has certain characteristics that define it as an individual, but at the same time functions as an integral part of a group, which cannot function without it. Steinbeck found this concept at work in his studies of marine biology, and so the concept lent itself liberally to *Cannery Row* and its marine biologist protagonist — a human application of a broader taxonomic rule. But there was already some evidence of this concept knocking around in Steinbeck's head in his earlier works. In *Cup of Gold* or *Tortilla Flat*, for instance, a person's individuality may suffer temporarily for his sacrifices to the group. With *In Dubious Battle* the sacrifice finally proves fatal. A crisis arises that far surpasses the others in gravity.

This gravity is deepened by the controversial nature of the subject matter at hand. By the 1930s, the U.S. had already gone through one "Red scare" during World War I and would go through another twenty years later, with the rise of Senator Joseph McCarthy and the House UnAmerican Activities Committee. The very mention of Communism was enough to make some politicians see red. In fact, Steinbeck was pilloried by people and groups as varied as Oklahoma Congressman Lyle Boten, school boards in New York, Illinois, and California, and both pro- and anti-Nazi groups for his labor novels. However, much of the traditional hostility toward Communism was ill-informed, with the average red-baiter likely to be unable to define Communism, let alone identify it in practice. In fact, with its central thesis of workers contributing to the system according to their ability and receiving from the system according to their needs, many might identify Communism, at least in its theoretical form, as the quintessentially American idea, where all people are considered inherently equal and opportunities are available to all citizens regardless of class, race, sex, or other potentially prejudice-inducing traits. This is why Steinbeck's choice of the theoretic "Grail" of Communism in this novel is so inherently American. Few countries have wrestled as violently against a system that could be said to have such a strong affinity to its own national identity. And though it can be said that it is Communism's requirement that the needs of the individual be subjugated to the needs of the group that poses such a threat to American sensibilities, this incongruity too is at the heart of Steinbeck's early Grail quests.

The strain on the metaphor at hand shows in the novel. For example, despite the presumably chivalric nature of any Grail-questing knight or group, the labor organizers and workers are far from chivalrous, Nolan's personal nature notwithstanding. Mac's remark to Nolan at Anderson's house at the orchard is telling: "How's it feel to be a party man now, Jim? It's well when you read about it — romantic. Ladies like to get up and squawk about the 'boss class' and the 'downtrodden working man.' It's a heavy weight, Jim" (*Dubious* 661-62). Elsewhere, Mac remarks sarcastically to Albert, "Haven't you got no idears about the nobility of labor?" (*Dubious* 712). This second remark is particularly significant because of the underlying assumption that labor is, in fact, *not* noble, particularly when one has seen it up close. Equally ignoble, however, are their opponents, who, as Mac points out more than once, are often drawn from the ranks of the American Legion. Ironically, in a late work, *America and Americans*, Steinbeck would lump groups like the American Legion together with fraternal lodges and Masonic organizations as emblems of the knightly aspect of American social life (*America* 89-90). Clearly much would change in the twenty years between these two works.

As we have already noted, Steinbeck's journalistic research on migrant workers yielded, after *In Dubious Battle, Of Mice and Men* and *The Grapes of Wrath* in rapid succession. World War II brought a new set of challenges to Steinbeck, with work commissioned by the Roosevelt Administration and front-line reportage for the *New York Herald*, not to mention screenwriting work in Hollywood (the screenplay to the war-tinged *Lifeboat* is among his works) and his popular success with *Cannery Row*, which itself arose from Steinbeck's burgeoning interest in marine biology. Even before these efforts, he had done his part as a citizen before the U.S. entry into World War II by celebrating Norwegian resistance to the Nazis in *The Moon Is Down*. However, despite these novel venues, Steinbeck's work would remain largely anchored in the Arthurian myth.

CHAPTER III

Raymond Chandler

It has become a basic critical assumption that Raymond Chandler used the Arthurian model in constructing his detective novels. However, the extent to which Chandler relied on the Arthurian myth has been somewhat underestimated. Chandler's early work shows clear signs of an interest in medieval topics, and much of the short fiction he wrote before completing his first novel, *The Big Sleep*, makes clear reference to the Arthurian tradition. By the time *The Big Sleep* was published, Chandler was able to construct a complex text with less obvious Arthurian allusions that carried strong cultural and even political associations. Chandler took care to include the Celtic and Irish aspects of these legends in *The Big Sleep*, and this attention implies a clearly anti-English agenda in the work — an agenda that is further illuminated in Chandler's non-fiction about the detective-fiction genre.

Chandler was born in 1888 in Chicago but moved to London with his mother when he was seven and stayed in England until he was twenty-three, when he settled in Los Angeles. During his British years, Chandler was educated at the Dulwich College Preparatory School and later studied in France and Germany. After his education was completed, Chandler took civil service examinations, and he briefly worked as a clerk before turning to a career in letters. Between 1908 and 1911, while still living in England, Chandler found employment translating works and writing essays and poetry for such publications as the *Westminster Gazette*, *Academy*, and *Chamber's Journal*. None of the verse written during this period shows much promise, but it does indicate that Chandler's medievalist proclivities as a writer developed very early. Jacques Barzun's observation that in this early work we may "find the germs of [later] attitudes" rings true (Chandler *Before Marlowe* x).

Some of the poetry merely establishes a medieval mood without

43

addressing themes of greater substance. For instance, the protagonist of "The Quest" recalls, "I wandered on the moorland and the fen" (*Before Marlowe* 14). Similarly, the narrator of "When I Was King" recalls "[t]he time I trod Valhalla / And chose my goddess out" (*Before Marlowe* 16). "Time Shall Not Die" contains this image: "And every knight comes riding light / Helm'd in a cypress wreath" (*Before Marlowe* 48). Other poems are more specific in addressing the themes of romance and chivalry that would appear in later Chandler works. For example, in "The Perfect Knight," the title character is described thus: "He hath a sword of altar fire, / He hath a shield of shimmering air, / The one to slay his base desire, / The one to guard him from despair" (*Before Marlowe* 24). Here we can see the beginnings of Philip Marlowe, who must guard simultaneously against the numerous femmes fatales who cross his path and against his own growing despair at a society gone to pot. One of the last poems Chandler published before returning to the U.S., "The King," places romance on the level of monarchy: "The lost waves moan: I made their song. / The lost lands dream: I wove their trance. / The earth is old, and death is strong; / Stronger am I, the true Romance" (*Before Marlowe* 47). Romance would continue to occupy a pivotal role in Chandler's work.

There is little evidence to suggest that Chandler did much writing at all between his return to the U.S. in 1912 and the appearance of "Blackmailers Don't Shoot," his first published short story, in 1933. During this period he worked as an accountant and served in World War I, attached to a Canadian Army unit. After the war, he returned to accountancy, becoming an auditor for an oil company. He married in 1924 and continued working in industry, eventually rising to an executive position, until he was fired in 1932 for absenteeism and drinking. It was at this point that Chandler turned to writing once again as a profession. He chose hard-boiled detective fiction as his genre and Dashiell Hammett, who had debuted in 1929 with *Red Harvest*, as his model — from which he would eventually depart.

"Blackmailers Don't Shoot" deals with a film producer being blackmailed with love letters that have gone missing. Through the resolution of the plot, a love triangle is exposed, a device, as William Marling notes, that will appear again and again in Chandler's work. "Blackmailers" opens with a description of the gumshoe, and this description, while not specifically evoking the image of a knight, is still somewhat chivalric, or at least heroic, in its approach:

The man in the powder-blue suit — which wasn't powder-blue under the lights of the *Club Bolivar* — was tall, thin, with wide-set gray eyes, a thin nose, a jaw of stone.... His clothes fitted him as though they had a soul of their own, not just a doubtful past. His name happened to be Mallory ["Blackmailers" 69].

The naming of the detective is Chandler's first Arthurian turn. (A minor character named Slippy Morgan — note the surname — also makes an appearance.) This turn is problematic, however. Mallory is a far cry from either the knights that the famous author of the (almost) same name created or even Thomas Malory himself, who had a peerage. For instance, as Jerry Speir has noted, for part of the story Mallory himself appears to be blackmailing other characters (*Chandler* 91). Nevertheless, he stands head and shoulders above the other people with whom he interacts — including lawyers, policemen, and corrupt politicians — in trying to determine who is blackmailing whom. In this way, Chandler begins to form the idea that the private eye is the last upholder of values in an increasingly corrupt system. For instance, while in police custody, Mallory takes issue with one of the policemen beating a suspect. Through such behavior, the gumshoe segregates himself from his surroundings.

The "goodness" of Mallory relative to his counterparts is further explored in Chandler's second short story featuring this private detective, "Smart-Aleck Kill." In this story, Mallory is again employed to foil a blackmailing scheme against a filmmaker. And once again, at the heart of the matter are men who would normally be upholding the law — here Councilman John Sutro, who is in cahoots with organized gangsters. In Chandler's short fiction, it is so rare for the detective in question to happen upon a character who is not thoroughly crooked that it is worth remarking when such an event takes place. For example, a later story, "Red Wind," features a pair of detectives, Ybarra and Copernik, who personify the concept of "good cop/bad cop." In one scene, the detectives have the detective Dalmas (renamed Marlowe in later editions) in custody during a murder investigation and the following exchange takes place:

> Ybarra said slowly: "What do you want?"
> Copernik's face convulsed and he slapped his long hard thigh. "This guy's good," he jeered. "He falls for a stray broad and breaks every law in the book and you ask him what does he want? I'll give him what he wants, guinea!"

> Ybarra turned his head slowly and looked at him. "I don't
> think you will," he said. "I think you'll give him a clean bill
> of health and anything else he wants. He's giving you a les-
> son in police work" ["Red Wind" 208].

Whereas we might normally expect figures of law enforcement to
embody certain ideals, here those ideals are lacking in one of the two
men presented. That the virtues are given not to the white officer but
to the Latino officer would suggest that in the period this story was written (it was published in 1938) the tables have turned even more than previously expected. Copernik is brutal and racist; Ybarra is well-mannered
and fair.

Another 1938 story, "The King in Yellow," is also significant for the
Arthurian imagery it evokes, beyond the medievalist flourish of the
story's title and title character. The story details the murder of a jazz
trumpeter, King Leopardi, and the discovery that he was killed by the
brothers of a woman he jilted some years before. The Arthurian connection is that one of Leopardi's steady gigs is at the Club Shalotte. Using
this name, Chandler brings to mind Tennyson's poem "The Lady of
Shalott," about the suicide of a woman betrayed by Sir Launcelot.
Chandler apparently draws an analogy between Leopardi and Launcelot
through the first letters of their names and their nobility (in Leopardi's
case, purely nominal). Chandler's primary innovation, however, is the
use of violence to "resolve" the situation.

One of the last stories Chandler published before releasing *The Big
Sleep* was "The Lady in the Lake" (later expanded into a novel of the same
title). The title alone reverberates with the Arthurian legends, with the
Lady of the Lake being any one of those women — alternately named
Nineve, Nimue, Vivien, or some similar name — who, depending on the
legend, give the sword Excalibur to Arthur and/or seduce Merlin, dis-
covering his powers and then imprisoning him forever in the bole of a
tree. In Chandler's version, however, the Lady is *in* the Lake: she is a
corpse discovered by private detective John Dalmas when sent on a miss-
ing-person search by a Los Angeles businessman.

Here we see one of the fundamental images in Arthurian mythology thoroughly debased by Chandler. If the Lady of the Lake is dead,
then Excalibur cannot reach Arthur's hands and many of the accomplishments of the Round Table are consequently nullified. That it was
another woman who killed the woman whose body is found in the lake
is a further profanation of the role of women in general in society. Once

held captive as damsels in distress, women are now the equals of men in their ability to take lives.

There are other Arthurian flourishes in this story. First, there is the character of Lancelot Goodwin — the man with whom the missing woman had allegedly disappeared. By using the name "Lancelot" for this character, Chandler keeps the tradition of Launcelot of cuckolder. "The Lady in the Lake" also introduces a Fisher King analogue in the character of Deputy Sheriff Tinchfield, who is one of the rare upstanding lawmen to be found in Chandler's work. Tinchfield is working the murder case of the woman found in the lake in his capacity as a law officer, but it is Dalmas, the private eye, who makes the real discoveries and ultimately uncovers the truth about the lady in the lake. In this sense, Dalmas acts as a knight in Tinchfield's service, just as Galahad or Percival act in this role for the Fisher King or Arthur, depending on the myth at hand. In place of the goal of revitalizing the king and, by proxy, the land, Dalmas will help to get Tinchfield re-elected.

The Big Sleep was published a few months after "The Lady in the Lake." Employing a technique that he would use time and again, Chandler constructed the novel by melding together two earlier short stories. Thus it is not surprising that there are essentially two plots in the novel. The pornography/blackmail plot is the central storyline, while the disappearance of Rusty Reagan is — for most of the novel, at least — the subplot. Similarly, there are two texts in the novel, roughly corresponding to each plot. On the one hand, the main text of the novel is a hard-boiled detective story in its classic form. The subtext of the novel, on the other hand, is an intricate interweaving of Celtic (and often specifically Irish) legend, folklore, and myth that share a connection to the Arthurian legends.

In constructing a novel with a strong Celtic influence, Chandler takes care to dismantle some of the traditional conventions that the general public most readily identifies with Arthurian legend. Chandler intended, as in the short stories, to debase such knightly codes as chivalry and *comitatus*, which were inextricably tied to Malory's work. For instance, when Marlowe first enters the Sternwood home, he sees a stained-glass panel showing a knight trying to rescue a damsel tied to a tree:

> The knight had pushed the vizor of his helmet back to be
> sociable, and he was fiddling with the knots on the ropes that
> tied the lady to the tree and not getting anywhere. I stood

there and thought that if I lived in the house, I would sooner
or later have to climb up there and help him. He didn't seem
to be trying [*Big Sleep* 3-4].

Critics such as Speir and Gay Brewer have pointed out that the panel
foreshadows Marlowe's rescue of Carmen Sternwood from the hands of
pornographers, but both critics are also careful to note that, in the long
run, Marlowe really does Carmen little good, as she is most likely fated
to spend the rest of her life in a home for the criminally insane for killing
Rusty Regan. She needs a doctor more than a knight (Fontana 181). In
this way, they contend, Chandler is showing the failure of chivalry to
achieve a happy ending in the modern world.

Similarly, the often-analyzed chess game that Marlowe plays against
himself serves as another example of the failed chivalric code. Returning
to his room, Marlowe finds Carmen naked in his bed, and as he contemplates her, he also contemplates a chessboard on a nearby card table,
on which he has laid out a six-move problem. He moves a knight, then
decides the move was wrong, declaring, "Knights had no meaning in
this game. It wasn't a game for knights" (*Big Sleep* 156). The double
entendre here is obvious: The solution to the problem on the board does
not involve the pieces designated as knights; and in dealing with the
Sternwood daughters, the knightly code of chivalry has little place. It is
an anachronism in the modern world (Marling 82).

The use of chess imagery has a long history in Chandler's work.
Marlowe's predilection for chess pops up in the aforementioned short
story "Red Wind" when Marlowe explains to a gunman that he doesn't
use his chessboard for games, but rather to set up problems ("Red Wind"
177). That Marlowe doesn't play against an opponent is significant, suggesting that only he himself is worthy of knightly combat; all other opponents are beneath the game, as evidenced by the gunman's ignorance of
its rules. Later in the story when the pieces are scattered during a scuffle,
the chessboard as a symbol of the chivalric tradition of combat is further debased — now even Marlowe cannot stick to the rules.

The opening lines of the novel *The Lady in the Lake* also summon
up chess imagery: "The sidewalk in front of [the Treloar Building] had
been built of black and white rubber blocks. They were taking them up
now to give to the government, and a hatless pale man with a face like
a building superintendent was watching the work and looking as if it
was breaking his heart" (*Lady* 3). The dismantling of this large chessboard is an image along the lines of the scattering of the chessmen in

"Red Wind"—chivalric rules of combat no longer apply. Oddly, while Chandler changes the name of Lancelot Goodwin (from the earlier short story) to Chris Lavery for the novel version, thus effectively removing any specific Arthurian references in the work beyond the title, Chandler also changes Bill Haines' name from the story to Bill Chess. These changes perhaps suggest that while Chandler had begun to exhaust the Arthurian legend as a source by 1943, when *The Lady in the Lake* was published, he still considered detective fiction to be based on the imagery of courtly love and chivalry.

Returning to *The Big Sleep*, the destruction of the knightly code of *comitatus*—the code that dictates the bonds between knights and their king as being supreme over all others, including familial bonds—is played out in the relationship between Marlowe and General Sternwood. The initial problem in the relationship is that the general is hardly a strong figure worthy of knightly devotion. He is in poor health at the novel's beginning and there is every expectation that his death is imminent. He is a Fisher King character, like Tinchfield in the short stories but without the positive attributes. In addition, Sternwood is unable to control his children—an inability that highlights his overall weakness. As a result of the General's frailty, Marlowe lacks the central figure like that around which Malory's knights were able to build their identities. Marlowe becomes "a Bedivere without an Arthur" (Fontana 184).

The *comitatus* relationship between Marlowe and the General is also debased by the parallel relationships that Chandler offers in the novel. For instance, Carol Lundgren's loyalty to the pornographer Geiger has a *comitatus*-like quality, but it is obviously (in Chandler's mind, at least) adulterated not only by its criminal aspect but also by the homosexuality of the two men. Similarly, the hit man Canino displays a marked loyalty to Eddie Mars, but once again the criminality of the relationship far overshadows any positive aspect that we may perceive (Fontana 184-85).

Chandler does not abandon Malory's example entirely in *The Big Sleep*, however. Rusty Regan's mysterious disappearance is found to stem from a sort of love triangle between him and the Sternwood sisters. As noted above, the Arthurian love triangle among Arthur, Launcelot, and Guinevere is likely to come to mind, since it is one of the best-known in all of Arthurian legend. However, Chandler gives us reason to believe he is drawing instead from "The Book of Sir Tristram," the largest of the eight sections of the *Morte*, which tells a parallel story of love and betrayal. In "Sir Tristram," Tristan, a Knight of the Round Table, becomes involved in a love triangle with his uncle, King Mark of Cornwall (a Celtic land), and Isolde the Fair, a princess of Ireland, when Tristan and Isolde accidentally drink a love potion in each other's presence.

There are several clues that point to this story as an intertext for *The Big Sleep*. First, the Tristan and Isolde story contains a violent aspect that the Launcelot and Guinevere story lacks, as King Mark tries to kill Sir Tristan on several occasions. This action finds its parallel in Chandler's novel with Carmen's acts of violence, particularly her murder of Rusty. Second, in both "The Book of Sir Tristram" and *The Big Sleep*, the disputed lovers (Isolde and Rusty Regan) are Irish. Third, the love potion of the Arthurian story has its analogue in the alcohol and ether mixture that Carmen drinks to loosen herself up to pose for pornographic pictures, though in Chandler's version the sexual aspect is made primary. Finally, Chandler names the older of the Sternwood sisters Vivian. This name appears in, among other sources, Tennyson's *The Idylls of the King*, in which Vivien, an enchantress and one of the Ladies of the Lake, is a paramour of King Mark's. It is important to note that in Tennyson's work, Vivien tempts Merlin sexually and lures him into a hollow oak, where he is imprisoned for eternity. There is clearly some similarity between the names Merlin and Marlowe, and Vivian Sternwood makes several attempts at seducing Marlowe, at least partly to lead him astray on his quest for the truth.

While casting Marlowe in the role of Merlin may seem problematic as we simultaneously see him in a knight's role, like many American writers of Arthuriana, Chandler seems comfortable in having many of his characters play several symbolic or allegorical roles at once. For instance, another Arthurian role that Marlowe plays in *The Big Sleep* is that of Sir Gawain, particularly as the latter appears in the anonymous medieval poem *Sir Gawain and the Green Knight*. Ernest Fontana has pointed out that, like Gawain, Marlowe is tempted by a woman but does not submit to temptation, though he does accept a kiss (Fontana 181). Other clues to Chandler's inclusion of *Sir Gawain and the Green Knight* in *The Big Sleep*'s subtext are the copious references to the color green throughout the novel. For instance, during Marlowe's first interview with Vivian, Chandler is careful to have Marlowe note that she "flashed an emerald and touched her hair" (*Big Sleep* 18). Likewise, when Marlowe finds Carmen drugged and naked at the photographer's studio, he points out that she is wearing jade earrings (*Big Sleep* 35). These references to green jewelry are particularly significant in that they occur in moments of Marlowe's interaction with the two women who most enthusiastically attempt to seduce him.

Chandler's incorporation of subject matter from *Sir Gawain and the Green Knight* in *The Big Sleep* relates to the Celtic subtext of the novel in two ways. First, the beheading game that opens *Sir Gawain* has its roots in the gladiatorial games of ancient Ireland. Second, the afore-mentioned references to the color green in Chandler's work cannot help reminding the reader of those Celts best known for their "wearin' o' the green." There are other possible meanings for the use of the color green in the work. William Marling, for instance, contends that green is the color of desire in *The Big Sleep* (Marling 87). Meanwhile, Peter Wolfe posits that green is the color of destructive emotions (Wolfe 118). There is ample evidence to support either claim. However, Chandler is quite specific about the relationship of the color green to Ireland near the end of the novel, when Marlowe returns once again to the Sternwood man-sion and notes that "the lawns were as green as the Irish flag" (*Big Sleep* 209). This simile is just a small part of a distinctly Irish element that we will find in the Celtic subtext of the novel.

Although there is little similarity between their plots and characters, *The Big Sleep* also owes some debt to Edmund Spenser's *The Faerie Queene*, the massive epic poem that is infused with elements of the Arthurian leg-end. *The Faerie Queene* is Celtic in nature not only in that it glorifies the Welsh House of Tudor under which Spenser lived, but also in its juxta-position of the legends of King Arthur and the Celtic King Lear — a jux-taposition also to be found in *The Big Sleep*. Spenser's alignment of the myths occurs in Book II, Canto X of *The Faerie Queene*, wherein Arthur finds a history of the Britons in the library of Eumnestes that contains the story of Lear and his daughters (Spenser, II. X. 27–32). Literary histori-ans are quite certain that Spenser took his history from Geoffrey of Monmouth's own folk history, *Historia Regnum Britanniae*, which is the original source in England of both the Arthur and Lear legends.

Although there may be some doubt as to whether or not Chandler was familiar with the works of Spenser or Geoffrey of Monmouth, there is no doubt that he was familiar with Shakespeare. In fact, the original title for his later novel *Farewell My Lovely* was *Zounds, He Dies!* — a line by a minor character in Shakespeare's *Richard III* (Chandler *Raymond Chandler Speaking* 47). And as it so happens, *King Lear* is one of only two plays in Shakespeare's entire canon (the other being *Henry IV* Part 1) that makes specific reference to the Arthurian cycle. The reference in *Lear* can be found in the Fool's cryptic prophecy that ends Act III, Scene ii, when he states, "This prophecy Merlin shall make, for I live before his time" (III.ii.95).

The initial clue that Chandler is juxtaposing the Arthurian and Lear legends in *The Big Sleep* is the surname of the missing bootlegger, Rusty Regan. Once the paradigm suggests itself, it is not difficult to see General Sternwood as a Lear figure, with Carmen and Vivian playing the roles of Goneril and Regan, respectively. Their misdeeds negatively affect the ailing patriarch, but he steadfastly defends them to Marlowe and protects them from the blackmailers who mean to do them harm. Furthermore, like Goneril and Regan fighting for the attention of the evil Edmund, Vivian and Carmen vie for the affections of not only Rusty Regan, but of Marlowe as well. We can see how ineffective such efforts are, as in the following scene, in which the Arthurian and Lear references are most closely juxtaposed:

> "You're as cold-blooded a beast as I ever met, Marlowe. Or can I call you Phil?"
> "Sure."
> "You can call me Vivian."
> "Thanks Mrs. Regan."
> "Oh, go to hell, Marlowe." She went on out and didn't look back [*Big Sleep* 61].

Here Marlowe uses the surname with echoes in the Lear legend instead of the first name with echoes in the Arthurian mythology, at once casting Vivian into the evil-daughter role, reminding her that, unlike the Merlin of Malory and Tennyson, he won't succumb to sexual temptation, and also reminding Vivian that she is, after all, a married woman.

Viewing the novel with such a model in mind raises the question of who fills the role of Cordelia in the Sternwood family. The easiest answer is Rusty Regan, who seems more of a favorite son than a son-in-law to the General. Just as Lear's death immediately follows his discovery of the death of Cordelia, the discovery of Rusty's death by Marlowe leads him to meditate on the imminent death of General Sternwood, as he states in the passage from which the novel's title is taken, "And in a little while he too, like Rusty Regan, would be sleeping the big sleep" (*Big Sleep* 231). Furthermore, Marlowe assumes the role of France in the Lear model, acting as a sort of champion for Rusty and bringing (or abortively attempting to bring) the French courtly love tradition of chivalry into the whole scenario.

Perhaps the most subtle interweaving of Celtic folklore into the subtext of *The Big Sleep* involves the inclusion of elements of the Fenian cycle of Irish mythology. Once again, it is through the medium of Arthurian legend that we come to understand this cycle's place in the novel. In the Fenian legends, Finn MacCumhal loses his betrothed, Grania, a kinswoman of the King of Ireland, to his nephew, Diarmuid, when Diarmuid and Grania drink a magical potion in each other's presence. Scholars such as Roger Sherman Loomis have determined that the Tristan-Isolde-Mark love triangle from Malory developed from this original Fenian version:

> To clinch the matter, a Welsh text of the 16th Century tells a story of Tristan and Esyllt and March [sic] which exactly corresponds to the Irish saga of Diarmaid and Grainna [sic] and Finn. It was Ireland, then, which contributed the central theme of adulterous love to the tragic romance of Tristan [Loomis 80].

Since the love-triangle aspect of the Fenian cycle is the most readily applicable source for *The Big Sleep*, it could be said that Chandler was unaware of this cycle and that the true source was simply Malory. However, there are several clues that suggest the inclusion of the Irish source as well.

In the Fenian cycle, for example, Finn as a young boy steals a "salmon of knowledge" from another man and, while roasting the fish, burns his thumb. When Finn sticks the thumb in his mouth to ease the pain, he discovers that he gains wisdom by sucking the digit. Thereafter, whenever Finn is in need of extra wisdom, he sucks on his thumb (Gregory 14). Returning to *The Big Sleep*, if we note that, like Finn in the Finn-Diarmuid-Grania love triangle, Carmen occupies to some extent the same jealous position in the Carmen-Vivian-Rusty triangle, it seems suggestive that she too would have the habit of sucking and biting on her thumb, as when she first meets Marlowe: "She put a thumb up and bit it. It was a curiously shaped thumb, thin and narrow like an extra finger, with no curve in the first joint. She bit it and sucked it slowly, turning it around in her mouth like a baby with a comforter" (*Big Sleep* 6). Carmen is not receiving any supernatural wisdom through this action, however, though she *is* sucking her thumb for a certain kind of power — that is, sexual power over men, as her action is a sort of flirtatious simulation of oral sex (Simpson 88). As Lewis Lawson has pointed out, such a simulation is not without its negative side; in combining biting with sucking, she is approximating the Freudian *vagina dentata* (Lawson 750).

Other compelling clues to Chandler's incorporation of the Fenian cycle into the Celtic subtext of *The Big Sleep* can be found embedded in other characters. For instance, Rusty Regan is identified in the novel as having been a member of the Irish Republican Army and having "commanded a whole brigade in the Irish troubles back in 1922" (*Big Sleep* 123). Students of Irish history know that to have "commanded a whole brigade" in 1922, Rusty would have to have been involved in the republican movement for some time before then, and that before the "troubles" referred to, militant Irish nationalists were known as the Irish Republican Brotherhood, or by their nickname, the Fenians. Several smaller clues also exist, such as the aforementioned chess game (chess matches abound in the Fenian cycle as well as in the Arthurian legend), the shared madness of Finn MacCumhal and Carmen, and their shared blond hair.

Even the names of some minor characters call to mind the Fenian cycle. The chauffeur, Owen Taylor, has a first name that is an Anglicized spelling of the Irish name *Eoghan*, who is a character in the Fenian cycle. Insofar as Chandler never adequately explains the death of Owen Taylor, the character ends up seeming to the reader to be an afterthought at best. Such a shallow characterization seems to suggest perhaps Taylor's inclusion in the novel as a subtle clue to the subtext of the novel rather than as a fundamental contribution to the action of the work.

Furthermore, Marlowe tells General Sternwood at their first interview that he was previously employed by a Mr. Wilde of the Los Angeles Police Department. The reader cannot help thinking of that most famous Wilde, who was not only Irish, but who had a first name — Oscar — that was also the first name of Finn MacCumhal's grandson. The inclusion of a character with a surname readily identified with a homosexual scandal, coupled with the aforementioned love affair between Carol Lundgren and Arthur Gwynn Geiger (whose "Christian" names are modeled after the King *and* Queen of Camelot [Wolfe 117]) suggests a sexual ambiguity that helps explain Chandler's having taken the love triangles from both Malory's version of the Tristan and Isolde saga and the Fenian cycle, inverting the sexes of the principal characters in his own modern version.

Of the different strains of Arthurian legend running through *The Big Sleep*, the Irish sources definitely predominate. This emphasis did not go unnoticed by an Irish-American playwright named Eugene O'Neill, who borrowed Chandler's title metaphor for use in his own play, *The Iceman Cometh*. In emphasizing the Irishness of his subtext so strongly, Chandler is capitalizing on a political tension to expound on a literary tension that is germane to the genre in which he is working. In contributing to the development of the so-called hard-boiled detective story, Chandler — as well as his predecessor, Hammett — was assuredly working against the "formal" detective novel that preceded it. In constructing *The Big Sleep*, Chandler chose to reassert the Celtic aspect of the aforementioned Arthurian tales to offer a paradigm in which a literary genre may be wrested from its practitioners by its originators. After all, Arthurian legend, before its appropriation by Anglo-Saxons and Anglo-Normans as a national mythology, was the tribal folklore of the Celtic Gauls and Britons. Likewise, the detective story, before the dawn of Arthur Conan Doyle and his goddaughter Agatha Christie, was an American form, originated by Edgar Allan Poe.

Chandler adopts a specifically Irish point of view in his novel for several reasons. First and foremost, Chandler himself was of Irish heritage, as he pointed out in a 1945 letter to Charles Morton:

> I have a great many Irish relatives, some poor, some not poor, and all Protestants, and some of them Sinn Feiners and some entirely pro-British.... An amazing people, the Anglo-Irish.... I could write a book about these people but I am too much [an Irishman] myself ever to tell the truth about them [*Selected Letters* 41-42].

We should probably note first that there is no inherent conflict in being both Protestant and a member of Sinn Fein prior to the "troubles" of the 1960s. Among the prominent Protestant Irish republicans, for instance, was William Butler Yeats.

Returning to Chandler's letter, this excerpt reveals that Chandler thinks of himself as Anglo-Irish. This is an appellation made most popular by figures like Yeats, whose criticism, perhaps not coincidentally, was favorable of detective fiction (Steele 568-69), and who wrote several books on Irish mythology; and Lady Augusta Gregory, the chief patron of the Abbey Theatre in Dublin and the author of *Gods and Fighting Men*, a modern English retelling of the tales of the Fenian cycle. That Chandler was familiar with this politically charged ethnic term suggests a familiarity with the works of Yeats and Lady Gregory and thus provides a link between Chandler and the Irish cycle of mythology. (It also implies another connection between Chandler and Spenser, who became one of the earliest of the Anglo-Irish when he emigrated to Ireland in the sixteenth century.)

Furthermore, in pointing out that some of his relatives were members of Sinn Fein, the political arm of the I.R.A., Chandler shows an understanding of the tension between Britain and Ireland during this and previous centuries. Therefore, we might conclude that Chandler would consider a novel such as *The Big Sleep*, which is steeped in Irish influence, as a possible literary statement against the British, by way of lampooning their detective-story tradition. As a result, there are several pokes at the formal detective novel in *The Big Sleep*. For instance, the formal detective novel usually contains a puzzle of some sort at the center of the text. It could be a mathematical or cryptographical mystery, the solving of which requires the specialized analytical skills of the sleuth. In *The Big Sleep*, however, whenever Marlowe is presented with such a puzzle, he comes up short, as when he tries to crack the code of Geiger's client list:

> After that [a shower] I sat around the apartment and drank too much hot toddy trying to crack the code in Geiger's blue indexed notebook. All I could be sure of was that it was a list of names and addresses, probably of the customers. There were over four hundred of them.... Any name on the list might be a prospect as the killer. I didn't envy the police their job when it was handed to them [*Big Sleep* 42].

A night later, Marlowe is stumped again: "I took another look at [Geiger's] blue notebook, but the code was just as stubborn as it had been the night before" (*Big Sleep* 62). In the end, the code remains uncracked. This failure on Marlowe's part, coupled with his aforementioned failure to solve the chess problem, implies the futility that Chandler feels in solving such neat and tidy little puzzles when lives are hanging in the balance. Evidence of such views can be found in Chandler's famous essay on the art of detective fiction, "The Simple Art of Murder," wherein he writes, "There are also a few badly scared champions of the formal or classic mystery who think that no story is a detective story which does not pose a formal and exact problem and arrange the clues around it with neat labels on them" ("Simple" 16).

Elsewhere in "The Simple Art of Murder," Chandler takes issue with other aspects of the formal detective story and its British proponents. Besides a protracted attack on English mystery writer A.A. Milne (perhaps better known in the U.S. for being the creator of Winnie-the-Pooh than for his detective stories) and the seven fundamental flaws in his work, Chandler makes several other jabs at the English and their literary tradition. For example, Chandler by turns notes the faults in the works of writers like Doyle and Christie and feels comfortable in closing one section of the essay with the observation that "[t]he English may not always be the best writers in the world, but they are incomparably the best dull writers" ("Simple" 11). Elsewhere, Chandler is less explicit in his attacks, as when he suggests that the sleuth in the formal detective novel inevitably ends up having to figure out "who tramped the jolly old flowering arbutus under the library window" ("Simple" 3), obviously playing on his reader's most ready association with the words "jolly old." Likewise, Chandler's reference to "what time the second gardener potted the prize-winning tea-rose begonia" ("Simple" 10) conjures up images of England, the land of Madame George and roses. In any case, the impression left with the reader is one of contempt, albeit a playful sort of contempt.

Chandler also directs his sling at what he dubs the American "pseudogentility" that aspires to the English model of detective fiction. One such attack has its roots in *The Big Sleep*, when Marlowe finds himself in confrontation with Wilde, his former employer, and the gumshoe throws his hands up in despair, telling Wilde:

> Geiger's method of approach puzzled me and still does. I'm not Sherlock Holmes or Philo Vance. I don't expect to go over ground the police have covered and pick up a broken pen point and build a case from it. If you think there is anybody in the detective business making a living doing that sort of thing, you don't know much about cops [*Big Sleep* 213].

Besides restating the futility of the formal detective story's puzzle tradition, Chandler in this scene makes reference not only to a detective created by an English author (Doyle's Holmes), but also to an English-style detective created by an Anglophilic American author (Willard Huntington Wright's Vance). Chandler must have found the attack on

Vance's creator important, as he makes reference to Vance in "The Simple Art of Murder" as well. He goes on in the essay to suggest that, instead of trying to match the English in their capacity for boring readers or insulting their intelligence, American mystery writers should aspire to the greatness of the American Hammett, whose style was not wholly his own, as Chandler contends, but was instead an evocation of the "American language." Chandler considers Hammett in relation to the tradition of American realism and to such contemporaries as Ernest Hemingway, building a notion of literary nationalism of which the hard-boiled detective novel is an integral part.

This being said, one fundamental question regarding Chandler's own detective novels remains: If the hard-boiled detective is indeed an American form, then why would Chandler so carefully imbue his work with Irish/Celtic source material? The answer probably can be found in the special relationship between America and the Irish. For many decades, America has been the home of more people of Irish descent than Ireland itself, and this is certainly the most important tie between the two nations. With regard to the hard-boiled detective novel in particular, Richard Slotkin has written that the form's development is linked to Allan Pinkerton's famous detective agency and its crushing of the Irish-American railroad labor union known as the Molly Maguires. Though this would seem to forecast a less-than-ideal relationship between the Irish and the hard-boiled detective novel, Slotkin is careful to point out that in cracking the Maguires case, Pinkerton hired an Irish-American detective named McFarland to infiltrate the union, thus establishing a legitimate link between the gumshoe and the Irish masses (Slotkin 97–98). (The most accessible link between the Pinkertons and the hard-boiled detective novel, however, probably remains Hammett's tenure in the agency before he launched a literary career and aligned himself with the political left.) The connection between the Irish and law enforcement gained greater strength with the increasing Irish-American representation on the police forces of American cities. This phenomenon is reflected in *The Big Sleep* in two references to Marlowe as a "shamus." Only in America, home to both Jews and Irish, could a Hebrew, and later a Yiddish, word (*shamash*) meaning "caretaker" and pronounced SHAW-mish come to mean "detective" and be pronounced like *Seamus*, the Irish equivalent of "James."

The link between Ireland and America is also strengthened by the anti-colonial feeling against England in both countries, albeit in different eras, the U.S. having been founded upon British subjects' revolt against home rule, and Ireland having its own long history of colonial exploitation and subsequent revolution. While it is certainly true that there is little political philosophy to be found in *The Big Sleep*, the spirit of anti-colonialism can be found in the novel most readily in the surname of Chandler's detective. The best-known literary Marlowe is Joseph Conrad's sailor, who appears in *Heart of Darkness* and *Lord Jim*. The former work has often been cited for its inherent criticisms of British colonialism (Brewer 2). Through such an allusive character name, Chandler aligns himself with the anti-colonial Irish — not politically, but literarily, where Chandler perhaps believes it matters more.

Raymond Chandler's detective fiction from its very inception shows a keen interest in traditional Arthurian myth and legend, but in *The Big Sleep*, Chandler shows an equal interest in the minor Arthurian stories that are more Celtic in flavor. Drawing on Malory's "Book of Sir Tristram" from the *Morte*, and *Sir Gawain and the Green Knight*, Chandler drops clues to his reader that there is a Celtic subtext beneath the hard-boiled detective novel that forms the primary text. In this way, Chandler positions himself among such American writers of Arthuriana as Steinbeck, as we have already seen. And like Mark Twain, Chandler is using Arthurian material — albeit some material with a decidedly extracanonical flavor — to make a decidedly American statement against Britain, though Chandler's statement is less hostile and less political than Twain's. Chandler's age when World War II broke out (he was over fifty) kept him out of the draft, and the war had little effect on his work. However, the war would draw in John Steinbeck, and more importantly, it would act as an influence on a whole new generation of American writers of Arthuriana.

CHAPTER IV

Writers in World War II

The cataclysm of World War II affected all areas of American life. Literature and arts were no less changed than the spheres of politics and diplomacy, and the use of the Arthurian myth was no exception. America's principal Arthurian author, John Steinbeck, worked both as a war correspondent for the *New York Herald Tribune* and as a propaganda writer for the administration of Franklin Roosevelt, turning out essays on policy and promoting the Army Air Corps to the public. While Steinbeck's Arthurian leanings were necessarily subjugated to some extent during the war years, the Arthurian spirit was alive elsewhere, both in the cultural mainstream and in the political extremes. Hal Foster took the title character of his *Prince Valiant* comic strip on campaigns against thinly veiled representations of Adolf Hitler's Germany and Benito Mussolini's Italy, while American Führer William Dudley Pelley used the same mythos to promote National Socialism in the U.S.

An excellent barometer of public opinion during any conflict, global or local, is popular culture. Accordingly, Hal Foster's most famous comic strip, the Arthurian *Prince Valiant,* offers the insights of one purveyor of popular culture designed to appeal to a broad readership: comic strips in the 1930s and 1940s were not geared toward children only.

Foster himself was born not in the U.S. but in Nova Scotia. He arrived in Chicago in 1921 to attend art school and stayed in the U.S. until his death in 1982. (He stopped drawing *Prince Valiant* in 1971.) Before creating *Prince Valiant*, Foster made his debut as a professional cartoonist in 1929 with *Tarzan*, based on the work of Edgar Rice Burroughs. He introduced *Prince Valiant* in February 1937 as a color weekly.

It should be emphasized that the relationship between *Prince Valiant* and Arthurian mythology is tangential, though it is stressed throughout the history of the strip. Val, as the Prince is known, is a native not of Camelot but of Thule, a Germanic kingdom. However, his travels (which include more than one jaunt to North America, then populated only by natives) include several visits to Camelot, and Arthurian characters also appear outside Camelot. Immediately before the period of the strip discussed here, Val applies to become a member of the Knights of the Round Table but is turned down by Arthur because of his age. In a departure from virtually every other version of the Arthurian myth, Camelot does not fall in *Prince Valiant* and there is no death of Arthur. However, as we shall see, some aspects of the Arthurian legend, such as the doomed love of Tristan and Isolde, do appear in the strip, as does much of its imagery.

It is notable that when *Prince Valiant* first appeared, Europe had been dealing with the increasing menace of Nazi Germany for at least four years. Hitler had remilitarized the Rhineland and was making territorial demands against Czechoslovakia. Within the borders of the Third Reich, the Nuremberg Laws of 1935 had stripped Germany's Jews of citizenship and deported many, and greater horrors were soon to follow. Europe seemed to be preparing for war once again.

Foster, as well, seems to have been preparing for war in Europe as the Huns, one of the recurrent enemies in the history of the strip, first appeared in *Prince Valiant* in the spring of 1939. In this first episode, Attila the Hun has sacked Rome and southern Europe is under the control of the Huns. This can be seen as a reference to the political and military control that Hitler exercised over Mussolini, who had modeled his Fascist Italy on Rome under the Caesars, right down to the symbol of the *fasces*, an axe bound in wooden rods.

Germans had been known colloquially and pejoratively as "Huns" by other Europeans and by Americans since World War I, and with the atmosphere in Europe rapidly deteriorating toward war in 1939, the epithet was renewed. No better evidence exists that Foster intended the Huns to represent the Nazis than an undated drawing from Foster's notebook (see Figure 1) that shows Prince Valiant, having bested a Hitler in a Hun outfit, saying, "You poor dumb Huns have always started trouble that you've never been able to finish!" (Foster *Companion* 43).

Val forms a legion of Hun Hunters, which, in keeping with the Arthurian flavor of things, Tristram and Gawain join. Soon the legion numbers some 7,000 men, and though they are outnumbered by a Hun army of 20,000 led by Karnak the (obviously deliberately misnamed)

Figure 1: Hitler as a Hun drawn by Hal Foster. (Reprinted with special permission of King Features Syndicate.)

Invincible, they are victorious. When this series of strips was running, between January and May of 1940, World War II had already begun and Hitler and Joseph Stalin had partitioned Poland, but an unofficial cease-fire was in effect, since neither Britain nor France had yet moved against the Nazis. Thus, these strips can be seen as a morale-building series, showing as they do that even when outnumbered the righteous may conquer the evil.

The next step for Val, Gawain, and Tristram is to visit Hun-occupied Rome. Along the way, just as Arthur does in the second section of *Le Morte d'Arthur*, Val encounters and defeats a giant. In the next series, the three knights help a community of Italians build a small town away from the menace of the Huns. (Foster tells us this city will eventually become Venice.) Finally, before arriving in Rome and being greeted by the last Roman general, Flavius Aetlus, they help a jewel merchant recover some gems looted by the Huns. Soon after the knights meet Flavius, however, he is murdered by the emperor, Valentinian III, whom Foster has rendered to bear considerable resemblance to the similarly bald contemporary dictator of Italy (see Figure 2).

Figure 2: Valentinian drawn by Hal Foster to resemble Mussolini. (Reprinted with special permission of King Features Syndicate.)

Soon after the assassination of Flavius, Valentinian himself is assassinated. Once again, Foster seems to be both reflecting contemporary occurrences in Europe in the strip and providing morale-boosting narratives. Mussolini, like Valentinian, was an autocrat who could have a popular general put to death if he so desired. However, Foster shows with Valentinian's own fall that even the autocratic ruler may be deposed or defeated. In this case, Foster was particularly prescient, since Mussolini was in fact deposed by his own army in 1943.

The violent atmosphere in Rome forces Val, Tristram, and Gawain to part company. Gawain heads toward Marseilles, Val towards Naples, and suitably, Tristram goes back to Britain to pursue Isolde. From Naples Val sails to Sicily, and after a series of encounters with creatures both normal and extraordinary, ends up en route to Jerusalem, where he intends to recover the Singing Sword, which has been stolen by Angor Wrack. This sword, not mentioned in traditional Arthurian mythology, was, according to the strip, forged by the same wizard who created Arthur's sword, Excalibur, and is its twin. (The Singing Sword seems to have been grafted onto the Arthurian legend after its introduction in *Prince Valiant*. For example, one of contemporary fantasy writer Jack Whyte's Arthurian-based novels is entitled *The Singing Sword*. Similarly, when Warner Brothers followed up their successful Bugs Bunny short *Knight-Mare Hare* — in which Bugs takes the rôle of the Connecticut Yankee — with another medieval-themed short, they offered *Knighty-Knight Bugs*, in which Bugs played a court jester ordered to recover the Singing Sword from the Black Knight.)

Val's quest for the Singing Sword takes him to Jerusalem, where he recovers the sword and dedicates it to the pursuit of justice at the Holy City's Church of the Holy Sepulchre. These scenes suggest a possible solidarity on Foster's part with Jews who had fallen under the iron heel of the Nazis. Jerusalem — that most Jewish of cities — is an unusual choice of settings for *Prince Valiant*, particularly during a period when the latest persecution of European Jewry had already been going on for nearly ten years and, with the invasion of the Soviet Union by Nazi Germany, had turned extremely violent. Indeed, the chronology of *Prince Valiant* places Jerusalem not under Muslim administration or under the rule of medieval Crusaders but rather under the control of the Byzantine Empire, since the strip is dated to be contemporaneous with the putative reign of Arthur in the fifth century A.D.

After the Jerusalem episode, Val's travels for a time follow the Allied campaign. He sails west from the Holy Land along the northern coast of Africa where, during the winter of 1941-42, Allied soldiers were fighting the Nazis' Afrika Korps. Val encounters Gawain again in Gaul (France), where he is being held captive. As Gawain is a Knight of the Round Table and is thus characterized by Foster as noble, this kidnapping can be seen as a comment on the occupied state of France in 1942, when this series was running. Val's ability to free Gawain is perhaps another bit of morale-boosting on the part of Foster. Upon Val's return to England and Camelot, he helps thwart an invasion by the Vikings, another Germanic people. This sequence ran from the summer of 1942 through the winter of 1943, but the British had already managed to repel a Nazi invasion of the British Isles in 1940, so any historical reference by the strip here is questionable. In fact, for the remainder of the war, little of the material in *Prince Valiant* corresponds to contemporary events.

There is little question, however, that Foster's Huns were stand-ins for the Nazis, and his contributions may well have helped maintain morale for some. In a broader sense, Foster's *Prince Valiant* inspired a slew of Arthurian comic strips, beginning with the war-time comic-book hero the Shining Knight, who bowed in 1941.

Reaching an even broader audience during the war was Steinbeck, whose novel *The Moon Is Down*, about the Norwegian resistance to Nazi occupation, won broad acclaim. Steinbeck went to work for the government's Office of War Information in 1942 as a news editor, and while in this position he was approached by Army Air Corps General Henry "Hap" Arnold, who asked him to write what would become *Bombs Away*, an account of the formation and initiation of a bomber squadron. The choice of Steinbeck as propagandist for the government must have seemed ironic to many, given the frequent, though unfounded, attacks on him as being a Communist, or at the very least a Communist sympathizer, based on *In Dubious Battle* and *The Grapes of Wrath*. And while it is true that Roosevelt's administration differed greatly from the previous administrations that Steinbeck had been attacking, it was still not friendly to so-called Reds.

While *Bombs Away* is far from impressive artistically, it is interesting in the present context as even here Steinbeck could not avoid the imagery of chivalric knighthood that had characterized his writing from the very beginning. Much of the work is concerned with justifying the abandonment of World War I–style dogfighting for the style of a World War II bombing team. His rationale proves stunningly medieval:

> [B]ombing did not develop colorfully enough to overshadow in the public mind those silver knights who met in single combat over the line while men looked on and cheered the victor and buried with full honors the vanquished, whether he was friend or enemy, and set his propeller over his grave. It was the ultimate in romantic combat, complete with trappings and roaring steeds and audience…. The pilot was king [*Bombs* 112].

Reading such a description allows the reader almost to forget that fighter pilots like Manfred von Richtofen and Eddie Rickenbacker were actually killing people and not just jousting.

To maintain to a certain extent the legacy left by World War I flying aces, Steinbeck is quick to remind us that the pilot is still brave and true of heart, but it also becomes equally important to remind readers that this pilot relies very much on the crew that surrounds him. To this end, Steinbeck devotes a chapter of *Bombs Away* to each member of the crew, and in this way, he taps into the "group-man" concept of men in battle that he had already begun to develop in *In Dubious Battle*. Alan Brown reminds the reader of *Bombs Away* that the group-man idea "attempts to play down individualism so that men can learn to function as a unit" ("From Artist" 216). Still, with his chapter divisions, Steinbeck does give each crew member his moment in the sun. As Jay Parini notes, "*Bombs Away* develops in a particular way the generalized theme of allegiance to a group for the benefit of its individual members…." (*Steinbeck* 269). For instance, the ball turret gunner is given mythical status by Steinbeck, who notes, "There are already Paul Bunyans among our gunners and there will be more" (*Bombs* 70, 72). (Note that, while most of *Bombs Away* is in keeping with Steinbeck's traditional medievalism, here he opts for the distinctly American Paul Bunyan myth.)

This American flavor shows forth elsewhere, too, as when Steinbeck credits the Second Amendment to the U.S. Constitution and its purported right to bear arms for the prowess of ball turret gunners: "Luckily for us, our tradition of bearing arms has not gone from the country, and the tradition is so deep and so dear to us that it is one of the most treasured parts of our Bill of Rights—the right of all Americans to bear arms, with the implication that they will know how to use them" (*Bombs* 30). At other times, Steinbeck is almost jingoistic in his portrayal not only of the bomber crew but of the role of the U.S. in the war, as when he writes, "The Air Force proves the stupidity of the bewildered Europeans, who seeing this nation at peace, imagined that it was degenerate, who seeing that we fought and quarreled in our own politics, took this indication of our energy as a sign of our decadence" (*Bombs* 4-5). He is equally hard on isolationists in the U.S., however, noting, "Some of our leaders wished to cut the world in half—to defend this hemisphere against the other—while others thought it would be good business and good thinking to give England the weapons to fight the war for us" (*Bombs* 14).

Equivocations notwithstanding, Steinbeck was patriotic about U.S. involvement in World War II, and when he'd finished *Bombs Away*, he joined as a news correspondent one of the first British squadrons to penetrate Axis-held territory—first in North Africa and then into Italy. Though security reasons prevented him from mentioning it in any of his reportage, one of the officers with whom Steinbeck traveled was the actor Douglas Fairbanks Jr. The articles Steinbeck sent to New York from the front were eventually anthologized in the collection *Once There Was a War*, and while there is little in that volume to reflect it, witnessing combat first-hand was traumatic for Steinbeck. After a cease-fire allowed him to leave Italy, he immediately returned to California—and to writing about subjects other than the war. Warren French has suggested that, by setting *Cannery Row* before U.S. involvement in the war began, Steinbeck sought to avoid the subject of the war altogether (French *Revisited* 97-98); but the phantom of war remains, as in *Cannery Row*'s Chapter 14, with its soldiers in uniform visiting the Marine Station.

Steinbeck's thoughts turned to 1940, when he accompanied his marine-biologist friend Ed Ricketts on a specimen-collecting expedition into the Gulf of California. He had written about it in 1941's *Sea of Cortez*. In 1943, when he was back in Monterey, his association with Ricketts picked up where it had left off, and Steinbeck set to work on *Cannery*

Row, whose principal character, Doc, would be based largely on Ricketts. Ten years after *Cannery Row*'s publication, Steinbeck wrote, "In this climate [Ed Ricketts' laboratory] odd stories and odder characters abounded and I began to write them down — some real, some fancied. Out of this material I built a kind of folklore in conscious imitation of the tales of the Middle Ages, which have so colored our literature and our thinking" ("Dreams" 1). Steinbeck could not have made his medievalist intentions more clear.

One simple way in which Steinbeck drew on *Le Morte d'Arthur* in *Cannery Row* was to develop a narrative with numerous episodes and characters, while keeping a core of perhaps a half-dozen characters and a main storyline. All told, there are forty-six characters in what is really a slim volume, and several of the chapters are what critics have labeled "intercalary," that is, they do not do anything to advance the main plot. Typical of these kinds of characters and episodes are the scenes involving the Malloys, the poor couple who live in a boiler in a vacant lot and rent out the pipes as bedrooms. The similarity of their name to "Malory" may suggest a degradation of Malory's work by Steinbeck on some general level, but their inclusion in the narrative seems rather to suggest the depressed economic circumstances of the times. On the other hand, the inner circle of characters, besides Doc, includes Mack, Hazel, Gay, Dora, and Frankie, each of whom has a specific analogue in the Arthurian tradition.

The early chapters of *Cannery Row* concern the acquisition of the Palace Flophouse from its owner, the grocer Lee Chong, by Mack and his gang of men, who essentially take over the building to use as their own. Later, Mack will draw a chalk line around the bed of each of the men who live in the flophouse and threaten with a beating anyone who crosses those lines. As in the case of Danny of *Tortilla Flat* and the perhaps not coincidentally named Mac of *In Dubious Battle* (see Chapter 2), *Cannery Row*'s Mack takes on certain characteristics of the legendary Arthur: He is the de facto leader of a group of men gathered in a sort of Camelot who have a Round Table of chalk-ringed beds — though in *Cannery Row*'s case, each one is its own Siege Perilous (Timmerman 159), rather than just the seat of the knight bound for Grail questing. Perhaps the general absence of a Grail quest in *Cannery Row* is the reason for the generalization of the Round Table here.

The early chapters are also important because they explicate the Taoist background of Lee Chong, which informs much of the novel, and what Steinbeck called its "is" thinking — a sense of living in the moment. Steinbeck saw in his relationship with Ed Ricketts much of this kind of "taking it as it comes." Taoist "is" thinking combines with Steinbeck's concept of the "group-man" and the character of Doc to reveal the novel's basic themes and tie the novel to the Arthurian tradition as practiced in America. As seen in previous chapters, the character of Merlin as depicted in American literature (with the exception of Twain) is often highly attuned to nature and naturalism — recall the model of the Aeolian harp or the Merlin of *Cup of Gold* who dwells in the Welsh countryside — rather than a supernatural magician who can bend spoons. Doc plays the former role in *Cannery Row*.

Chapter 6 of *Cannery Row* offers a convenient comparison between the group-man ethos of Mack's Knights of the Round Table and the nature-centered thinking of Doc's Merlin. In this scene, Doc and Hazel, one of Mack's boys, are in the Great Tide Pool together. Doc is there to collect specimens for his experiments; Hazel has come along to help and because he enjoys Doc's company. Hazel is described in a somewhat knightly manner: "He was twenty-six — dark-haired and pleasant, strong, willing, and loyal" (*Cannery* 33). Hazel and Doc get into a conversation concerning Henri, who has been building a boat for the past seven years. Hazel says, "I think he's nuts." Doc replies:

> You don't understand…. Henri loves boats but he's afraid of the ocean…. He likes boats…. But suppose he finishes his boat. Once it's finished people will say, 'Why don't you put it in the water?' Then if he puts it in the water, he'll have to go out in it, and he hates the water. So you see, he never finishes the boat — so he doesn't ever have to launch it [*Cannery* 37].

Hazel can't understand this kind of "is" thinking; as one of the metaphorical Knights of the Round Table, he has to be goal-oriented. So he concludes again, "I think he's nuts."

The character of Gay is also alluded to in this chapter, a man who will soon be moving to the Flophouse because his wife beats him. This is a unique position for a man presumably to be depicted as a knight. Indeed, Gay is the only member of Mack's crew to even have a regular relationship with a woman — dysfunctional though it may be. The rest of the Boys find their "entertainment" at Dora's whorehouse. In that his central conflict is over a woman, Gay resembles several characters in the

Arthurian myth. In fact, he will be posthumously cast as Arthur himself (who had his well-known troubles with Guinevere) in the sequel to *Cannery Row, Sweet Thursday* (see Chapter V). For the moment, it is sufficient that Gay, through his conflict with his wife, comes to represent either Sir Launcelot or Sir Tristan—both knights of highest valor brought low by troubles with the fairer sex.

Returning to the Tide Pool, the differences between Doc and Hazel in this chapter points to the larger conflicts that arise in the novel. Mack and the boys will attempt to cheer Doc up from his mild depression—which itself is merely a fact of life and nothing that needs to be "corrected"—by throwing him two parties, both of which end disastrously. The tension reflects a similar tension in the Arthurian cycle between the Knights of the Round Table and Merlin. Malory is able to alleviate this tension rather easily by dispensing of Merlin very early in the *Morte*. But Steinbeck makes his Merlin his protagonist and renders him unable to disassociate himself from the Round Table. In the Arthurian cycle, Arthur acts as the mediator between the Knights and Merlin—if only for the short time that both forces exist simultaneously. In *Cannery Row*, Mack, who is the Arthur figure, tries to act in the same way but fails miserably.

What Steinbeck implies by thus elevating Merlin above Arthur and the knights is his point of view, at this time in his development as an author and a man, that "is" thinking is superior to other forms of thinking, and the only suitable method of dealing with the caprices of life. Take, for example, Doc's discovery in Chapter 18, when he is collecting specimens at La Jolla, of the body of a dead girl. We should recall that it is also while collecting specimens that Doc has previously demonstrated to Hazel "is" thinking in the case of Henri. We should also note that it is in such environments that Doc feels most comfortable. Taking this into account, Doc's comfort should be deeply disturbed by the horror of his morbid discovery. His response is quite different, however: "Goose pimples came out on Doc's arms. He shivered and his eyes were wet the way they get in the focus of great beauty. The girl's eyes had been gray and clear and the dark hair floated, drifted lightly over the face. The picture was set for all time" (*Cannery* 105). This is hardly a horrified reaction. Instead, it reflects the ability to adjust to the virtual Tao that Doc embodies as a naturalistic Merlin. As Robert Hughes concludes, Doc "acts as a spokesman for the values the novel upholds, bringing together the moral and the ecological strands of Steinbeck's thinking" (Hughes 120).

The single most Arthurian image in *Cannery Row* is an onyx clock surmounted by a bronze figure of St. George fighting the dragon. The retarded boy, Frankie, attempts to steal this object as a gift for Doc at one of his "parties." Steinbeck describes it through Frankie's eyes:

> The dragon was on his back with his claws in the air and in his breast was St. George's spear. The Saint was in full armor with the visor raised and he rode a fat, big-buttocked horse. With his spear he pinned the dragon to the ground. But the wonderful thing was that he wore a pointed beard and he looked a bit like Doc [*Cannery* 162].

According to our paradigm, Frankie is wrong in associating St. George with Doc, but perhaps this mistake can be attributed to his compromised mental state. It is also possible that, because Frankie eventually attempts to steal the clock, is caught, and is institutionalized, Steinbeck is implying that Frankie's association is incorrect. In either case, thanks to Spenser's *Faerie Queene*, the image of St. George and the Dragon is inextricably tied to Arthurian legend, and its inclusion here merely strengthens the other underlying Arthurian elements in the text.

Finally, as Howard Levant shows, "is" thinking is, by definition, non-teleological thinking, and this aspect of the philosophy is suggested by the non-resolution of the novel. At its conclusion Doc is no more (or less) happy than he was at the beginning, despite two parties planned for precisely that purpose. In fact, the final image of the novel is of Doc weeping. It is important to note that what has brought him to tears is reading the Taoist poem "Black Marigolds," a favorite of his. The poem is one of memory that weighs positive and negative images of the poet-narrator's loved one and is thus an apt text for a man like Doc, who is virile but alone, though perhaps not (yet) lonely. With *Cannery Row*, Steinbeck made a bold new Arthurian statement about the American concept of Merlin and his place in our society.

Just as Steinbeck was being recruited to fight National Socialism, there were forces within the U.S. borders seeking to promote fascism, and they were also using Arthurian myth to do so. The connection between the Arthurian cycle and fascism is well documented. Germany's famed nineteenth-century composer, Richard Wagner, popularized the Grail quest with his *Parsifal* and at the same time promoted an anti-Semitic agenda that would form the basis, in part, of Hitler's National Socialism. It is no coincidence that Hermann Göring's *Luftwaffe* would play Wagner's "Flight of the Valkyries" during the *Blitzkrieg*. On a more personal level, Hitler had a close relationship with the Wagner family, including a rumored affair with one of Wagner's daughters and a sort of foster fatherhood to Wagner's grandson. One of Wagner's sons-in-law was Houston Stewart Chamberlain, one of the "scientists" on whom Hitler based much of his theory of "race."

According to an interview that Wagner's great-grandson gave in 1998 to the *Irish Times*, his grandmother, who had loved Hitler, called him a "holy Grail" for Germany. While the Nazi regime was purposely ambiguous in its embrace of both Christian and pagan religious symbolism, a symbol like the Grail conveniently extends into both arenas, as much a Christian icon when represented as Jesus' cup at the Last Supper as a pagan relic as it appears in Wolfram von Eschenbach's *Parsifal*, which Wagner used as a source for the libretto for his opera. In the late twentieth century, Stephen Spielberg would depict the Nazi desire to capture religious relics, including the Grail, in his Indiana Jones films. There were, in fact, clear links between the *Ahnenerbe* within the Reich's Department for Pre- and Early History, and occultists within the Nazi Party (Campbell 215-16). The Nazi preoccupation with things Arthurian was not lost on their American sympathizers.

By coincidence, a 1975 essay on Steinbeck by Warren French mentions Clarence Brown's 1922 film *The Light in the Dark*, alternatively known as *The Light of Faith*, which tells of the finding of the Grail in 1920s New York and depicts its ability to heal an ailing woman with a simple touch (French "Use of Malory" 4). The principal figure behind the production of *The Light of Faith*, whom French neglects to mention, is Brown's co-screenwriter, William Dudley Pelley, who adapted his unpublished short story for the film.

Pelley's political career is of greater interest to the contemporary scholar than is his career in films: In 1933, Pelley founded the first National Socialist party in the U.S., the Silver Legion, in emulation of Adolf Hitler. His new party included an S.S.-style paramilitary group called the Silver Shirts. Unfortunately, there are few sources of information about Pelley's life and work that are not either his own autobiography, *The Door to Revelation*, self-published in 1939, or hagiographies written by later white separatists or self-styled "racialists" who never knew him. Historian Leo Ribuffo is one of the few mainstream scholars of political polarization between the wars to speak about Pelley at any length.

Throughout his entire political career, Pelley never abandoned writing, and like Steinbeck, he never abandoned Arthurian imagery or
medievalism in general. For example, Ribuffo details the hierarchy of
positions within the Silver Legion, some of which have strong echoes in
the chivalric tradition:

> An impressive-sounding officer corps commanded the rank
> and file: the Chief [Pelley], Chamberlain, Quartermaster,
> Sheriff, and Censor at national headquarters; a Commander,
> Adjutant, Purser, Bailiff, and Solicitor at state level; and a
> Chaplain, Scribe, Almoner, Marshall, and Advocate at each
> local post.... Elaborate regalia and hierarchy gave the Chief
> a 'Great Thrill' while also serving an organizational purpose
> [*Old Christian Right* 72].

Pelley's medievalism also found expression in aspects of his personal life, such as his claim to having been descended from Sir John
Pelley, who he says was knighted by Queen Elizabeth I (Pelley *Door* 3).
Similarly, Pelley details in his autobiography his views on chivalry for
one of his wives, Lillian — views that are surprisingly progressive for a
man so enamored of reactionary politics: "Coddling a woman's weaknesses, defending feminine indolence or lassitude, championing an intelligence that has all the brilliance and flexibility of cement, glossing over
petulancies, that's never Chivalry. You're but making such women
flabby" (*Door* 171).

Ribuffo notes, as does Pelley himself, that his early political views
were far from fascist; the young Pelley, born in 1890, was a utopian socialist whose views were based largely on Edward Bellamy's novel *Looking
Backwards*. In his first venture into publishing, a magazine called *The
Philosopher*, Pelley expressed sympathy for the working classes while pro-
fessing mainstream Protestant values, calling Jesus of Nazareth "Comrade
Christ" in one article. In his early twenties, Pelley entered politics, stump-
ing for a French-Canadian candidate for mayor of Chicopee,
Massachusetts. According to Pelley's autobiography, when his candidate,
running on a temperance ticket, was revealed in a newspaper operated
by the candidate's political rivals to have made clandestine deals with
breweries, a friend slammed the rival newspaper on Pelley's desk and said,
"That for your Galahad out of Quebec!" (*Door* 57). This ironic statement
is apparently the first significant reference to the Grail-questing knight in
Pelley's life, though it would not be the last. Pelley's appropriation of Grail
imagery illustrates the political polarization of the 1920s and 1930s.

While he had been quite successful publishing many of his short stories—not only in his own publications, but in mainstream publications with larger circulation, such as *Ladies Home Journal* and *Redbook*—Pelley's story "White Faith," about the Grail, was turned down. In his rejection letter, Karl Harriman, Pelley's editor, made reference to the most famous medievalist author, stating that the American people would have no use for "a story premised on the appearance in America of the *Holy Grail* of Tennyson's poem and working wonders in this twentieth century" (Pelley *Door* 178-79; emphasis original). Instead, Pelley was referred to a movie agent whom he identifies as Larry Giffen, who offered him $5,000 for the rights to make the story into a silent film starring Lon Chaney. The result was *The Light in the Dark*.

The plot follows a young woman with the Arthurian name of Elaine (Hope Hampton), who arrives in a boarding house in New York also inhabited by Tony Pantelli (Chaney), a petty thief. While Elaine goes job-hunting, her estranged boyfriend, Warburton Ashe (Elmo Lincoln), finds the Holy Grail in an Abbey in southwest England. A report of his find appears in the New York newspapers just as Elaine falls ill from an unnamed malady. Tony has never heard of the Grail, so Elaine tells him the story of how "Galahad, the purest Knight of the Round Table" quests for the Grail and how the "White Knight" fights his way and finds the cup, which glows in the dark as if to prove its holiness. When Elaine falls asleep, Tony looks through her purse and finds Ashe's business card and decides to find Ashe and confront him about his estrangement from Elaine. When Tony finds Ashe, he ends up punching him out and stealing the Grail, taking it back to Elaine. The cup glows when the lights are turned out, and Elaine is healed by touching it. Tony, meanwhile, is on the run from the police, who track him down at the boarding house. He is confronted by Ashe in a night court, but seeing Elaine there, Ashe decides not to charge Tony. The couple is reunited, while a heartbroken Tony leaves the courtroom as the film ends.

Pelley writes in his autobiography that Chaney "had done such a magnificent job of acting that he had stolen the picture from its heroine" (*Door* 188). He also writes that he felt that, as an author, he was considered "the lowest form of life in Jewish movies" (*Door* 188) and had no say about how the final edit came out. Although the autobiography was written well after Pelley's adoption of overt anti-Semitism, this remark supports Ribuffo's theory that it was failure in Hollywood that contributed most directly to Pelley's hatred of Jews (*Old Christian Right* 46). Pelley himself attributes his opinion of Jews to his trip to Siberia in 1919, during the Russian Civil War, as part of a YMCA volunteer group giving support to troops fighting the Bolsheviks. It was here that Pelley claims he discovered the connection between Judaism and Bolshevism that Hitler would later give as one of many explanations for systemic anti-Semitism in Nazi Germany (*Door* 122).

The strangest turn in Pelley's career came in 1930, when he claimed that he had a religious out-of-body experience in which, for seven minutes, he was taken into Heaven and encountered a man whom he perceived to be Jesus. Significantly, Pelley claims to have been reading a book on medieval history when the experience occurred (*Door* 289) — a passage that was using Emerson's notion of the Oversoul in its argument:

> I had come to a certain page in Emerson's wondrous essay on the Oversoul. I had lowered my book.... What *was* the Oversoul?... Was there a vast, brooding Consciousness that wrapt [*sic*] all humanity in Its heart? I asked. I asked earnestly. I wanted an answer. I was not asleep. I was not expecting what dramatically transpired. *It seemed as though the entire club coach was filled with a Presence* [*Door* 315]!

We should note that Emerson's concept of the Oversoul is related to the transcendent creative process that he detailed in his Merlin poetry. Pelley wrote up his experience in *My Seven Minutes in Eternity With Their Aftermath*, which became a fundamental text in his spiritual/political movement. Significantly, one passage in *My Seven Minutes*, describing his return to his body, has a curiously medieval feel: "And as I paused, something awful closed about me! It seemed as though a great suit of clammy, cloying armor, a miasma of implacable sinew had shut around me" (*Seven* 25-26).

After the out-of-body experience, Pelley experienced renewed vigor that manifested itself in his founding in 1931 of the Galahad Press, his latest vanity press, from which he published his new magazine, *Liberation*. In his autobiography Pelley recounts the press's naming during the early years of the Great Depression, when he told an employee, "Heroic dilemmas require heroic remedies. We'll call it Galahad Press" (*Door* 353). Not surprisingly, *Liberation* became a major vehicle not only for Pelley's right-wing politics but also for screeds against the "Jewish-controlled" movie industry. Galahad Press was short-lived, however, as

Pelley was forced to liquidate its assets in 1932 to pay debts. His next enterprise, in 1932, was to take out a land charter in North Carolina and establish the Foundation for Christian Economics and Galahad College in Asheville. The school opened on July 5 and offered, as Pelley writes, "nine weeks of intensified studies in all branches of Christian mysticism" (*Door* 388). Pelley recalls, "In 1932, when my collection of sixty-five lectures delivered in fifty-days of Galahad Summer School in North Carolina covered the Unknown History of the World, my material was at hand in the depths of my own memory" (*Door* 46). While Christian Economics was based largely on Pelley's earlier Bellamy-influenced socialism, it also included anti-Semitic philosophy. In this sense, the economics preached at Galahad College was essentially National Socialist according to Hitler. When Hitler became Chancellor of Germany in January 1933, Pelley formed the Silver Legion in response. According to Ribuffo, "[Pelley] urged others ... to come forward and be valiant.... He pronounced Jesus a Silver Shirt ahead of His time. Jesus clairaudiently accepted the commission and echoed the call to 'Stand Forth as Knights'" (Ribuffo 63). We should note here not only that Jesus was now considered a far-right sympathizer as opposed to "Comrade Christ," but also that Pelley continued to use the trappings of medieval knighthood as part of his propaganda.

Around the same time, Sinclair Lewis published *It Can't Happen Here* with Pelley serving as a prototype for the American dictator, Berzelius "Buzz" Windrip. In the novel, Windrip writes these lines:

> I honor [Pelley] not only for his rattling good yarns, and his serious work in investigating life beyond the grave and absolutely proving that only a blind fool could fail to believe in Personal Immortality, but, finally, for his public-spirited and self-sacrificing work in founding the Silver Shirts. These true Knights, even if they did not attain quite all the success they deserved, were one of our most noble and Galahad-like attempts to combat the sneaking, snaky, sinister, surreptitious, seditious plots of the Red Radicals ... [Lewis 63–64].

Lewis and Pelley were old rivals, Pelley having taken personal offense at Lewis's depiction of small-town life in *Main Street*. He told one acquaintance that Lewis's novel was "a distorted, reprehensible libel on the American small town. I'm not only going to write an article ... about it, I'm going to do a book myself for answer" (*Door* 171). The book with which Pelley answered Lewis was *The Fog*.

Lewis wrote in *It Can't Happen Here* of Windrip challenging Roosevelt for the Presidency in 1936. Pelley did just that, garnering 1,600 votes that were restricted to Washington state. Nonetheless, Pelley was an avid and frequent assailant of Roosevelt's character and background, labeling him "Rosenfeld" and speculating on the Dutch-American Roosevelt's purportedly Jewish background. Among the publications Pelley produced was one called *Cripples' Money: Who Gets the Proceeds From the Presidential Birthday Balls?* The implication made by this pamphlet is that money raised at yearly presidential fundraisers for infantile paralysis (or polio), by which Roosevelt was himself paralyzed, never reached its charitable destination (*Cripples* passim). Given Pelley's self-expressed Galahad image, it is not difficult to see his campaigns against the wheelchair-bound Roosevelt as a variation on the Fisher King myth, wherein the physically (often sexually) wounded king's power is diluted, and so a knight must find the Grail to restore the land. Here the knight (Pelley) is seeking to overthrow the king, but the end goal of restoring vitality to the country — in this case, the Depression-scourged U.S. — is the same.

Although Roosevelt could withstand all the personal attacks that Pelley and other far-right agitators like Father Charles Coughlin and Gerald L. K. Smith could throw at him, once Britain went to war with Nazi Germany and Roosevelt needed popular support for the Lend-Lease Act and later for full-scale war against the Axis powers, he could not brook the kind of dissent that Pelley fomented. Ribuffo terms the Roosevelt Administration's reaction to the reactionary right wing in the years before the U.S. entry into World War II a "brown scare," writing, "Like 100% Americans' during the Red Scare of 1919-20, liberals and radicals during the 1930s founded or redirected organizations specifically to combat subversion — in this instance, far right subversion" (*Old Christian Right* 178). As a consequence of this brown scare, Congress passed the Smith Act in 1940, instituted the House Un-American Activities Committee in 1938, and prosecuted Pelley for sedition as a co-defendant in *United States v. Gerald Winrod*. Pelley was convicted in 1942 and jailed until 1950, when he was paroled on condition that he neither write nor engage in political matters.

Pelley spent his last years writing so-called Soulcraft poetry that delved into his purported religious experiences, and much of this poetry retains the medievalist flavor of his earlier writings. For example, the final stanza of "New Concord Bridge," an attack on Marxism (as Pelley conceived it), reads: "Arms stale in armor, adulate the cause / Of dreams made Deeds, that carnage-furies cease! / Soon we start back, all campaigns won, from wars / For mustering out in Groves of Etheric Peace!" Similarly, Sir Jesus of Nazareth makes a reappearance in "The Goodly Company," which begins, "This Knighthood dubbed, O Lord, by Calvary's Blade." And "Purple Heart" asks a series of chivalric rhetorical questions, such as, "Who strides these years as the Knight of Tears yet kindles our pride again?" (*Twilight Clear*)

Pelley died in 1965, a marginal figure in the history of literature, film, and politics. His only relevance to mainstream politics was a statement by Jimmy Carter when running for the presidency in 1976 that, although he was a Bible-believing Christian, he was *not* the kind of Christian that Pelley was (Ribuffo 270). As an epilogue, several of Pelley's colleagues went on to become major players in the white supremacist movement in the U.S. Gerald L.K. Smith, mentioned above, was a prominent Ku Klux Klan leader through the segregation battles of the 1950s and 1960s. One of the Silver Shirts, Richard Butler, is currently the head of Aryan Nations, a Christian Identity organization based in Hayden Lake, Idaho, that boasts one of the largest memberships among American neo-Nazi organizations. And the Arthurian myth in particular continues to play an important role in extremist politics, exemplified in the Excalibur Society, a National Socialist organization formed by American Nazi leader Harold A. Covington when he was living in self-imposed exile in Britain.

From center, right, or left, the Arthurian myth has continued to be a source of inspiration for American writers. With Allied victory in the war came economic well-being and a return to normal life in the U.S., as exemplified by the 1950s. *Prince Valiant* started the absorption of Arthurian material into popular culture that remains to this day, with the strip still in circulation and a large number of mass-market fantasy novels touching on Arthurian themes. As Frederick Karl has pointed out, however, the Fifties were very much a "counterfeit decade" that held within it all the social strain that would eventually rise to the surface during the Sixties (Karl 176). Pelley certainly appreciated this fact, as the thinly veiled criticisms of American society in his Soulcraft poetry show. Similarly, Steinbeck would continue to critique American culture and values in his postwar work, though with a slight change in perspective regarding the ultimate possibility of redemption available to the country.

CHAPTER V

Steinbeck's Later Works

Cannery Row brought Steinbeck renewed success as a commercial author, allowing him to return to writing fiction with renewed vigor. Besides the short fiction collected as *The Pearl* and *The Red Pony*, Steinbeck dabbled again in film, providing the screenplay for Elia Kazan's film *Viva Zapata!*, and wrote the "novel-play" *Burning Bright*. With 1952's *East of Eden*, Steinbeck experienced his greatest critical success since *The Grapes of Wrath*. With the next novel, *Sweet Thursday*, a sequel to *Cannery Row*, Steinbeck returned to the Arthurian mythos as a source for inspiration. Here, as well as in his final novel, *The Winter of Our Discontent*, and in his modern-English Malory project, we find the third and final stage of Steinbeck's development as an Arthurian writer. In this period, Steinbeck's work is characterized by a new optimism in which, despite the recapitulations of moral questions raised in earlier works, there is also a renewal of faith in the ability of human beings to improve their own lot, and, as a consequence, the world at large.

The genesis of *Sweet Thursday* was Steinbeck's idea, encouraged by his friend, composer Frank Loesser, who had written the music for the highly successful *Guys and Dolls*, that *Cannery Row* could be adapted into a stage musical. Steinbeck found libretto writing difficult, however, and he concluded that he would be better off writing a straight novel—a sequel to *Cannery Row*—and then letting more experienced musical writers take the project from there. Given this goal, it is not surprising that *Sweet Thursday* lacks the serious undertones of its predecessor, and this lighter constitution extends to the novel's characters and to its use of Arthurian motifs and symbolism. As in the earliest of his novels, in *Sweet Thursday* Steinbeck is once again effecting a Grail quest for his characters—this time with Hazel playing the part of the Grail knight and Doc filling the role of the Fisher King.

As noted in Chapter II, Doc's role in *Cannery Row* is as a sort of Merlin in the naturalistic tradition of American literature. But while it is true that Steinbeck chose to recycle many of the settings and characters of *Cannery Row* in *Sweet Thursday*, the characterization of Doc changes to such an extent that his Arthurian precedent shifts. For example, in the first novel Doc's association with naturalism finds expression in the tidepool experiments he performs, while in this novel Doc is suffering from writer's block and is unable to produce any publishable research. In this way Steinbeck distances Doc from science and thus from the Merlin prototype of the earlier work. Removing Doc from the necessarily unstable realm of naturalism, with its inherent group-individual tension, enables Steinbeck to use him as the subject of the novel's principal boy-meets-girl plot device. Whereas previously such pursuits would have seemed beneath Doc, now they form the center of the novel.

In his analysis of *Sweet Thursday*, Richard Astro focuses on the character of the seer — the mysterious, unnamed character who appears in Doc's lab from time to time, offering philosophical observations. It appears that Steinbeck has shifted all the Merlin symbolism from Doc to this character. Astro calls the seer "an idle dreamer," and, citing Peter Lisca, author of one of the earliest book-length studies of Steinbeck, states that the seer has "shifted the ground of his metaphysics 'from mystic concepts of the unity of all life to the doctrine of romantic love, which he prescribes for Doc'" (Astro 210). Therefore, even as the character of Merlin is pushed to the sidelines in this novel, Steinbeck finds it nonetheless necessary to profane this Arthurian character by having his project be part of the larger, mundane project of finding a companion for Doc, not to mention Steinbeck's casting of a seer as a mild kleptomaniac who steals candy bars for his nourishment (Timmerman 177).

Although Doc can no longer serve as a Merlin figure, this does not mean that he is rendered in entirely superficial terms. Rather, taking on certain aspects of the mythical Fisher King, Doc now appears spiritually wounded, with the source of his wound being his loneliness. Still, as in previous Steinbeck novels, there are no simple character-for-character associations between the dramatis personae of *Sweet Thursday* and the Arthurian pantheon. For instance, Louis Owens suggests that the Fisher King character in *Sweet Thursday* is not Doc but Mr. Deems, the effigy that the Row's inhabitants burn yearly. Owens writes, "In this idyll the Christ figure, a sacrificial entity appearing throughout Steinbeck's writing in manifold guises as Christ, hanged god, and fisher king, is drastically reduced.... With Mr. Deems the heavy inheritance of *The Waste Land* is acknowledged and, for the moment at least, cast aside ("Critics" 197-98). Whether Steinbeck intends Doc, or Mr. Deems, or both to represent the Fisher King in the novel, Owens's reference to Eliot here is instructive. As was the case in the early novels, particularly, as noted above, in *Tortilla Flat*, *The Waste Land* acts as a sort of anxiety-producing influence on Steinbeck's worth as an Arthurian author. Just as Danny and his retinue in that novel were World War I veterans and thus shared with Eliot's personae the scars of battle, Doc, as well as several other Cannery Row denizens, has served in World War II. In fact, it is a distinct possibility that his loneliness results from a kind of spiritual wound he received in combat. In this sense, he is very much like the Fisher King, whose wound is also, in some versions, quasi-romantic (i.e., sexual) in nature. We will see how Eliot's influence on Steinbeck continued in *The Winter of Our Discontent*, with Owens's references ringing true again. Furthermore, as Howard Levant writes, the war had wider consequences, including the decline of the canneries of the title with the fish being taken out of the water to feed troops and the massive population shift in California because of troop mobilization (Levant 260).

Owens also points out that the novel's title indicates a departure from Arthurian elements typical to Steinbeck's work. *Sweet Thursday* implies "'the day *before* Good Friday,' ... that part of our mythic history free of the burden of the Christian sacrifice, free of that weight of responsibility" ("Critics" 198). One possible way we can see this symbolism is that any Grail associations in the novel are drawn from the relic as the chalice Jesus used at the Last Supper, rather than as a receptacle for Jesus's blood when His side was pierced as He hung on the cross on Good Friday.

Owens links the absence of Easter symbolism here to the absence of an Arthur figure in the novel, identifying as the Arthur figure Gay, one of Mac's gang at the Palace flophouse who has been killed in the war. We can see the connection between Gay and Arthur in a representative passage: "No one had ever been allowed to sit or sleep in Gay's bed. He might return one day, the boys thought, even though he was reported dead, and his Army insurance paid" (*Sweet Thursday* 2; Owens 198).

While Dora, the proprietor of the local whorehouse, has been replaced in *Sweet Thursday* by Fauna, and while storeowner Lee Chong has sold out to Joseph and Mary Rivas, Gay has no replacement. And like Arthur in Avalon at the end of the *Morte*, there is the suspicion that

Gay may return. However, because of the symbolic dating of the story here to precede Easter, not to mention Steinbeck's requirement that he stay anchored in reality, we can rest assured that Gay will not be returning. The role of Arthur, therefore, will remain vacant. Mac, though the leader of the "knights" of the Row, is really more of a sort of Launcelot than an Arthur. We should also note that here is another resonance with Eliot's *Waste Land*, with the tragedy of war in the background.

Notably, then, the Grail quest in *Sweet Thursday* takes place neither during the traditional Pentecost season as per Malory nor in the fall, when the Grail quest of *Tortilla Flat* occurs. As noted above, Hazel, the retarded member of Mac's crew, acts as the Grail knight here. One indication of Hazel's role comes when Mac's boys dress in costumes from *Snow White and the Seven Dwarfs* for the masquerade ball on Cannery Row. This scene certainly inspired V.S. Naipaul's observation that in *Sweet Thursday* Steinbeck had "turned the Row into Fairyland" (Naipaul 163; Parini 377). At the very least, it is a gentle jab at medievalism. Hazel takes the role of Prince Charming. Describing his costume, Steinbeck notes, "An Elizabethan ruff of stiff paper was around his neck, and on his head a Knight Templar's hat with a white ostrich plume. From his belt around his middle hung a long scabbard. His right hand proudly held a cavalry saber at salute" (*Sweet Thursday* 183). Besides the obvious medievalist flourish of the costume as a whole, the detail of the Knights Templar hat is significant. In several sources, notably Wolfram von Eschenbach's *Parsifal*, the original Templar order is associated with the guardianship of the Holy Grail. Though the hat here is merely an icon of the Masonic order of the same name, the association is clear. As we shall see, this same hat will make a similarly symbolic appearance in *The Winter of Our Discontent*.

From the outset, by making his Grail knight a developmentally disabled man, Steinbeck is once again debasing the Grail quest, as he did earlier in *Tortilla Flat*. Just like Galahad in the *Morte*, Hazel is predestined to become the Grail knight, as implied when Dora tells his fortune for him, informing him that he is destined to become the President of the United States. Thus the symbol of the Siege Perilous in Malory, the seat of the Round Table that bears Galahad's name as the place of the knight who will obtain the Holy Grail, is translated in *Sweet Thursday* into a crystal ball prediction of a highly unlikely event. Similarly, Steinbeck makes Hazel's relative suitability as a Grail knight even more explicit in an early draft of the novel's introduction, when he has Hazel state that he had an uncle who was a deputy sheriff (Owens 201). In this way, Steinbeck gives Hazel a knightly genealogy, just as Galahad was Launcelot's son; though changing Galahad's noble pedigree to an indirect ancestor who was a mid-level civil servant is just another profanation of the Grail myth, both expressing the universality of the myth and making it more mundane.

As already established, the Grail that Mac's knights and, in particular, Hazel will obtain is a girlfriend for their Fisher King, Doc. This relationship carries further debasements with it, since Suzy, the woman they pick, is a prostitute, albeit an inexperienced prostitute. Not since *Cup of Gold* has Steinbeck's use of a woman as a Grail representation been so apparent, but here the ambivalence of the project found in that first novel is gone, and this simplicity is indicative of a larger shift in Steinbeck's use of Arthurian imagery and motifs in expressing aspects of the human condition. Whereas in the earlier novels the elusive nature of men's goals founds expression in abstractly signified Grails that brought little if any happiness when they were finally brought home, the securing of a girlfriend for Doc results in a happy ending for the book, complete with an offer for Doc from his friend Old Jillingballicks of a teaching and research position at the California Institute of Technology, and, of course, the finishing and publication of his previously languishing research paper.

To return to Hazel, his fitness as a Grail knight is further compromised by his first action in pursuit of his Grail: On the order of Mac, he breaks Doc's arm so that he will be out of his lab for a few days and Mac's gang can arrange to surprise him there with Suzy when he returns. Then, in Chapter 32, aptly titled "Hazel's Quest," Joe Elegant, Steinbeck's stand-in in the novel, explains to Hazel the true nature of Doc's problem and how it needs to be solved:

> Joe Elegant scowled faintly at the interruption. "Distill the myth and you get the symbol," he went on. "The symbol is the paper he wants to write, but that in itself has impurities, needs distillation. Why? Because it is a substitute, that's why. His symbol is false. That's why he can't write his paper. Frustration! He has taken the wrong path. And so he brings in false solutions. 'I need a microscope,' he says. 'I need to go to La Jolla for the spring tides.' He will not go to La Jolla. He will never write his paper."
>
> "Why not?"
>
> "Wrong symbol. We must go back to the myth, the sea. The

> sea is his mother. His mother is dead but she is living. He is
> carrying treasures from his mother's womb and trying to save
> them. Do you understand?"
> "Sure," said Hazel listlessly.
> "He needs love. He needs understanding," said Joe Elegant.
> "Who don't?" Hazel asked [*Sweet Thursday* 208-09].

Much of Joe's analysis is too esoteric for Hazel to understand and some
of it is incorrect, but the basic message — that Doc needs love more than
anything else — is fundamentally true. And, in a sense, by putting into
Elegant's mouth words concerning myth and symbol, Steinbeck is
telegraphing to his reader the true meaning of Doc's dilemma, not to
mention how it will eventually be resolved. In this way, the simplistic
nature of Hazel's quest is underscored here. Hazel has been made to
understand what he needs to do, and like the knight he believes himself
to be, he carries out his duty.

Sweet Thursday was eventually turned into a musical; it was produced on Broadway in November 1955 as *Pipe Dream*, with Rodgers and
Hammerstein handling the music and libretto. Ironically, despite the
obvious lightness of *Sweet Thursday*, Steinbeck was surprised that the
story appeared in the musical as "an old-fashioned love story." Steinbeck
wrote to Oscar Hammerstein, complaining, "[T]hat is not good enough
to people who have looked forward to this show based on you and me
and Dick [Rodgers]" (Steinbeck & Wallsten 1989 505; Parini 385). The
critics responded badly as well, though the show ran for 246 perfor-
mances thanks to advance ticket sales and low production costs. The
show closed in June 1956. Biographer Jay Parini writes, "The failure of
Pipe Dream brought to an end Steinbeck's fascination with the theater
as a vehicle for his imagination" (*Steinbeck* 387).

Steinbeck's next novel, *The Short Reign of Pippin IV* (1957), carried
many of its own medievalist associations, particularly because of the
main character's ancestry among the Carolingian rulers of medieval
France. There is little if any significant use of Arthurian motifs in that
novel, however. But, after publishing *Pippin*, Steinbeck traveled to
England, where, at the invitation of the great Arthurian scholar Eugene
Vinaver, he was given access to the newly discovered Winchester manuscript of Malory's *Le Morte d'Arthur*. It was on Vinaver's work on the
Winchester manuscript that Steinbeck would base his modern English
rendering of the *Morte*, and he worked on the project through much of
1958 and 1959. Illness then forced Steinbeck to return to the U.S., and

once he was stateside again, he wrote *The Winter of Our Discontent*, his last novel.

Steinbeck worked on his Malory project more or less in the same order established by Malory. The six parts of the first tale of the *Morte*, "The Tale of King Arthur," were "translated" first, with Steinbeck's interpretation generating a much larger number of words than the original — an indication of how much was added by Steinbeck, particularly in terms of characterization. The second tale — Malory's "Tale of the Noble King Arthur That Was Emperor Himself Through the Dignity of His Hands," which tells the story of Arthur's defeat of the Roman Emperor, Lucius, and thus the acquisition of the empire — is omitted entirely by Steinbeck. No less an Arthurian scholar than Eugene Vinaver wrote that Steinbeck left out the Lucius section because it was "far too archaic to lend itself to the same treatment that Steinbeck had given the other sections" (Simmonds "Note" 26).

Steinbeck finished his rendering of the third tale, that of Sir Launcelot, and then put the project down in 1959, though at later dates he did some work on the fourth tale, concerning Sir Gareth of Orkney, before he died. Of these pages he wrote to his agent, Elizabeth Otis, "I think I have something and am pretty excited by it but I am going to protect myself by not showing it to anybody so that after I get a stretch of it done, if it seems bad, I can simply destroy it" (*Acts* 364). But they were to remain unfinished and unpublished. Thus the meatiest tales in the *Morte*, those of Tristan and Isolde and of the quest for the Holy Grail, received no treatment at all by Steinbeck, but it is reasonable to assume that this would have resulted in hundreds more pages and a far less cohesive — albeit finished — final product.

John Gardner, in his review of Steinbeck's modern English rendering of Malory when it was published in 1976 as *The Acts of King Arthur and His Noble Knights*, wrote primarily about Steinbeck's "translation" method, noting that the author went far beyond simple interpretation, often adding his own material. As an example, Gardner pointed out that the scene in which Merlin leaves Camelot to travel with Nyneve and teach her the craft of sorcery runs a mere sixteen lines in Malory's original but covers two and one-half pages in Steinbeck's version (Gardner "*Acts*" 116). One curious way in which Steinbeck generates new material is by way of literary allusions to other Arthurian works outside Malory. For instance, in "Gawain, Ewain, and Marhalt," Steinbeck offers this familiar line as a segue from one scene to the next:

"When the sweet showers of April had pierced the roots of March, they came near to the trysting place where the path tripled to stamp the oath of quest" (Steinbeck *Acts* 173). The reference is to the first line of Geoffrey Chaucer's *Canterbury Tales*, but translated the same way Steinbeck has rendered Malory into modern English.

That Steinbeck chooses *The Canterbury Tales* is significant for two reasons: First, Chaucer's story cycle contains Arthurian material, notably The Wife of Bath's Tale; and second, Chaucer's opening line served as the inspiration for the first line of Eliot's *The Waste Land*, so the allusion has Arthurian echoes in both the medieval and modern spheres. Later, in "The Noble Tale of Sir Lancelot du Lake," Steinbeck writes, "Now as the Frensshe books say and Malory also, as well as Caxton and Southey, Sommer and Coneybear, Tennyson, Vinaver, and many others, Sir Lancelot continued on his way, overturning knights one after another, and the way to Arthur's court was thronged with defeated men paroled in Sir Kay's name to Guinevere" (*Acts* 274).

Beginning with the very Malorian reference to "the Frensshe books" (which he leaves untranslated), Steinbeck lists other important publishers and/or translators of Malory, including British Poets Laureate Robert Southey and Alfred Lord Tennyson, the latter of whose *Idylls of the King* inspired the Arthurian revival of the nineteenth century (see Chapter I). More curious is the mention of not only Caxton (the edition of Malory that Steinbeck first became familiar with) but Eugene Vinaver too. In this way, Steinbeck makes a clearly personal reference, dropping the names of the scholars who most influenced his own personal encounters with the Matter of Arthur. Indeed, that Steinbeck lists Malory himself as a source is probably indicative of his own immersion in the project, since he was using Malory as his prototype. Notably, Steinbeck suggested in a letter to Elizabeth Otis the title *The Acts of King Arthur and His Noble Knights*, remarking that this title would be a boiling down of the original title as presented by Caxton: *The Birth, Life and Acts of King Arthur, of His Noble Knights of the Round Table, Their Marvelous Enquests and Adventure, the Achieving of the San Greal, and in the End Le Morte d'Arthur With the Dolorous Death and Departing out of This World of Them All* (Steinbeck *Acts* 313). H.O. Sommer and F.C. Coneybear were also early editors of the Caxton text.

Mary Williams has written that one innovation of Steinbeck's is the characterization of women, and this change may indicate his sympathy with the most recent women's-rights movement that was just beginning as Steinbeck was working on his Malory project. Williams uses the "Gawain, Ewain, and Marhalt" episode as her example of Steinbeck's revision, noting that the woman each knight encounters has something to teach him ("Lessons" 40). Thus, by giving these three female characters moral and occupational dimensions missing from Malory, Steinbeck corrects what he saw as a generally negative attitude towards women on Malory's part, having noted in a letter to Elizabeth Otis, "Malory doesn't like [women] much unless they are sticks" (Williams "Lessons" 40; Steinbeck & Wallsten, 1989 *Letters* 351). For example, Steinbeck adds a moral dimension to the lady Ettard that is absent from Malory's characterization, having her upbraid Gawain for seducing her, thereby betraying both her and her true lover, Pelleas. Marhalt's unnamed counterpart is depicted by Steinbeck as being his equal. Williams writes, "He makes the fire; she boils the tea and prepares a meal. At night, he sleeps while she watches [stands guard]. Next day he ties a scarf around both of them so that she can sleep while riding pillion" ("Lessons" 40).

However, it is Ewain's companion, Lady Lyne, who is given the strongest characterization by Steinbeck. She is depicted as a woman actually able to teach knights how to fight, and she drills Ewain on fighting methods and equips him with weaponry. Typical of her advice is to say that the armor he is wearing is insufficient to protect him in combat: "Metal never takes the place of skill. It protects areas that need no protection" (*Acts* 177). Laura Hodges notes that Lyne is entirely Steinbeck's creation; Malory neither designates a name for Ewain's counterpart nor develops her character to any significant degree. Williams attributes Steinbeck's characterization to his reverence for his sister's companionship ("Lessons" 40).

If Lyne serves as a stand-in for Mary Steinbeck in the text, then Launcelot stands in for Steinbeck himself. The "Sir Launcelot du Lake" section represents the most concise portion of his "translation" of Malory. Nonetheless, it offers several examples of changes made by Steinbeck that indicate how he intended to give the text a twentieth-century relevance, and most prominent among these revisions is the personal relevance Steinbeck bestows upon the knight. There is little doubt that Steinbeck admired the character of Launcelot greatly; the author's addition of the epigram "And noble it is" to the title page of "Sir Lancelot du Lake" is proof of that (Steinbeck *Acts* 205). Hodges draws attention to another of Steinbeck's letters from the composition period, this one containing remarks on his affinity for Launcelot. "You see I *like*

Lancelot," Steinbeck wrote. "I recognize him ... in some ways he is me" (Steinbeck and Wallsten, 1989 795; Hodges "Psychodrama" 72). One way in which Steinbeck resembles Launcelot in his own way of thinking is in regard to the Grail quest. Steinbeck writes, "In himself [a writer] must fail as Lancelot failed — for the Grail is not a cup. It's a promise that skips ahead." Hodges goes on to suggest that, in ending his modern English rendering of Malory with the Launcelot tale, Steinbeck in essence resigns himself to his own imperfections.

Aside from Steinbeck's personal affinity for Launcelot, another notable change is found in Steinbeck's treatment of magic. While his modernization of the text by no means eliminates the use of magic and magic-using characters like Merlin and Morgan le Fay, he still renders magic as less supernatural and more mundane and thus less pervasive on the characters — and here on Launcelot — thus engendering a greater ambivalence toward the subject of magic in the text. For instance, Hodges notes that although Steinbeck retains from Malory Merlin's stature in the early part of the text as the principal guide to the young Arthur in consolidating his rule, Steinbeck "emphasizes the idea that Merlin's power to effect eventual political accord through his wisdom and magic is attacked and nullified by the power of love" (Hodges "Adaptation" 71). This is a powerful alteration on Steinbeck's part — the subordination of the power of magic to the effects of love — and, like the shifts in the characterizations of female characters, may reflect the influence of another incipient contemporaneous social movement, the "free love" movement. Thus the loss of Merlin to the magic of Nyneve — with whom he has fallen in love — is a poignant commentary on this subordination of magic to love. Steinbeck writes that Merlin "knew what was happening to him and knew its fatal end, and still he could not help himself, for his heart doted on the Damsel of the Lake" (*Acts* 99). Once Merlin has been imprisoned in the chamber in the rock, Steinbeck reiterates the magician's fatalism: "And Merlin remains there to this day, as he knew he would be" (*Acts* 101).

This characterization of Merlin as willingly playing a part in his own demise exists in Malory, but as rendered by Steinbeck it leaves a different impression of the magician than previous American writers of Arthurian literature have developed. Emerson had established a tradition of Merlin as the personification of nature captured in art, akin to an Aeolian harp. Similarly, Steinbeck had previously cast Merlin either in a similar role — in *Cup of Gold*, for instance — or as a human example of the group man — as seen in the characterization of Doc in *Cannery Row*. However, we have already seen earlier in this chapter that in *Sweet Thursday* Doc ceases to be a Merlin figure. This marginalization of Merlin in Steinbeck's Arthurian text continues in his rendering of Malory and is one of Steinbeck's most important innovations in Arthurian literature in America. However, it is not Arthur who fills the void left by Merlin's early demise in this text, as might be expected, particularly if we use Malory as an example. Instead, as we have established, Launcelot fills that role.

To continue with Steinbeck's treatment of magic, elsewhere he makes magic subordinate to plain old common sense. For example, commenting on the relationship between Ewain and Lyne, Hodges applies this subordination to Lyne's gift of a magic sword and magic armor to the knight: The only things that are fundamentally "magical" about these items are that the armor is smooth and light, thus allowing greater mobility while wearing it, and that the sword has been well-forged by "fairy" blacksmiths who have made sure that it has proper balance for easier handling (Hodges "Adaptation" 73). Hodges' most provocative assertion, however, is that Lyne's ability to prophesy is really just an early realization of "the downfall of chivalry and the evolution of a more effective method of warfare" (Hodges "Adaptation" 75). A conversation between Ewain and Lyne on the future of knighthood while in the presence of the peasantry brings this point home:

> "... Everyone knows no peasant will stand up to a noble knight, a man born to arms."
> "These [peasants] may learn. I know that it is as paralyzing to put war in the hands of a soldier as to place religion under the marshaling of priests. But one day a leader who puts victory before ceremony will lead these men — and then — no more knights."
> "What a dreadful thought," Sir Ewain said. "If lowborn men could stand up to those born to rule, religion, government, the whole world would fall to pieces."
> "So it would," she said. "So it will."
> "I don't believe you," Ewain said. "But for the sake of the discussion, what then, my lady?"
> "Why then — then the pieces would have to be put together again."
> "By such as these —?"
> "Who else? Who indeed else?" [*Acts* 184].

Steinbeck is here placing in Lyne's mouth one of the lessons he hoped to teach with this project: In a country like the United States, which has no hereditary nobility and where the equality of all citizens is presupposed, we must rely on all people to perpetuate chivalric values, not just the aristocrats.

Unfortunately, as *The Winter of Our Discontent* shows us, Americans much too often come up short in the quest for such values. Steinbeck developed this novel from an earlier short story, "How Mr. Hogan Robbed a Bank." Among many major changes between the short story and the novel, Steinbeck moves the action from Labor Day weekend in the story to two sections in the novel, taking place on two holidays, Easter weekend and Independence Day. Besides the clear associations with Easter that Steinbeck's Grail-inspired stories all have, using the Fourth of July allows him to associate the themes of this novel with generalizations about American society. In that vein, Steinbeck offered the following in place of the usual disclaimer against associating characters in the novel with real people: "Readers seeking to identify the fictional people and places here described would do better to inspect their own communities and search their own hearts, for this book is about a large part of America today" (*Winter* iv).

Despite its Shakespearean title, *Winter* is Steinbeck's most Malory-influenced work, with the exceptions of *Tortilla Flat* and the translation project; although it perhaps bears mentioning that *Richard III* (along with *King Lear*) is one of the very few plays in Shakespeare's canon that includes any references to the Arthurian cycle of mythology. John Timmerman offers ample evidence gleaned from Steinbeck's letters during the composition of the novel to suggest that the author's Malory translation project informed much of his thinking while writing *Winter*. For example, Timmerman cites a September 28, 1959, letter to Joseph Bryan, in which Steinbeck writes of the similarities between Malory's time and his own:

> It is my theory that Malory was deploring [fifteenth-century society] by bringing back Arthur and a time when such things were not so. A man must write about his own time no matter what symbols he uses. And I have not found my symbols nor my form. And there's the rub [Timmerman 257; Steinbeck & Wallsten, 1989 649-50].

Not only is there a Grail knight and a Grail object — in this case, a talisman that is a Hawley family heirloom — in *Winter*; there is also the

Malorian theme of betrayal, as well as a Morgan le Fay/Morgawse character in Margie Young-Hunt, who attempts to seduce Hawley.

One familiar piece of symbolism arises in the first half of the novel.
The novel's protagonist, Ethan Allen Hawley (the name itself being a
nod to the very American nature of the themes Steinbeck sought to
address here), returns from work to find his son, Allen, waiting for him
in his bedroom. Allen asks his father if he may borrow his sword and
hat from the Knights Templar Masonic society (*Winter* 72-73). If
Steinbeck's association of the Arthurian legends with these items were
not immediately apparent, he offers more evidence a few paragraphs
later, as if to make the matter certain. Looking through the books in his
son's attic room, Hawley finds a copy of Malory's *Morte* on the shelf:
"[T]he Morte d'Arthur of majesty with drawings by Aubrey Beardsley,
a sickly, warped creature, a strange choice to illustrate great, manly
Malory" (*Winter* 74-75). The juxtaposition of these images is important.
In the case of the hat and sword, the son who borrows the Knights
Templar costume is the same son who will be caught having cheated in
an essay contest. Regarding the Beardsley-illustrated edition of Malory,
Steinbeck seems to have Hawley making reference to Beardsley's homosexuality, with the implication being that having such a "sickly, warped
creature" illustrate what Steinbeck considered to be a book worthy of
using to instruct the young on morality was yet another debasement,
both of the myth and of society in his own time.

Later in the novel, the Templar hat reappears, when Hawley bumps
into Joey Morphy while taking the hat, the plume on which has yellowed
with age, to the dry cleaners. This image itself serves as another symbol
of the defilement of medieval myth, and specifically Arthurian myth, in
the novel. Just as the plume has yellowed, so have the ideals it represents
been compromised. Morphy expresses surprise when Hawley tells him
he is a Knight Templar, and Hawley responds, "It's in the family. We have
been Masons since before George Washington was Grand Master"
(*Winter* 141). Given the already established relationship between the
Knights Templar and the Arthurian cycle, Hawley's statement regarding the significance of freemasonry to Colonial Americans goes along
with the dating of the story and Hawley's own name to link Steinbeck's
themes to the American situation at large.

Michael Meyer links the characterization of Joey Morphy to Eliot's
Tiresias in *The Waste Land* ("Winter" 266), an appropriate comparison
if we consider that both men are able to predict the future (Tiresias is a

seer, while Morphy foresees his own downfall), but that both suffer from blindness, Tiresias's literal and Morphy's more figurative. However, *Winter*'s more apparent nod to Eliot comes when the flirtatious Margie Young-Hunt visits the Hawley home and conducts a Tarot card reading for Ethan, who as narrator recounts, "Then I saw strange cards — a tower riven by lightning, a wheel of fortune, a man hanging from his feet from a gallows, called *le pendu*, and Death —*la mort*, a skeleton with a scythe" (*Winter* 87). Two of the cards that Margie throws for Hawley appear in the tarot thrown by Madame Sosostris in the third stanza of *The Waste Land*:

> Here is the man with three staves, and here the Wheel,
> And here is the one-eyed merchant, and this card,
> Which is blank, is something he carries on his back,
> Which I am forbidden to see. I do not find
> The Hanged Man [*Eliot* 51-55].

Timmerman suggests that in the inverted position of the Hanged Man "religion is turned on its head in this world, in which traditional moral norms for value are replaced by commercial ones" (Timmerman 260). However, the meaning of this throw relative to the Tarot is also relevant. While the Hanged Man normally betokens bad luck for the person whose fortune is being told, when the card comes up inverted, the opposite meaning of the card, i.e., good luck, is foretold. Therefore, here we have a hint of how Steinbeck will choose to end the novel.

The reference to the Wheel of Fortune is a more obscure reference to an anonymous Middle English poem, *The Alliterative Morte Arthur*, a verse rendering of the Arthurian legend that Steinbeck referred to in a letter to Chase Horton while working on the Malory project (*Acts* 301). In one of two dream sequences in that poem, Arthur sees himself bound to the Wheel of Fortune along with several other historical leaders, and he sees that his own favorable position is about to change.

This card's image resonates in at least two ways in *Winter*. On one level, as Timmerman points out, the card is analogous to the scene in Baker's Bank, when Hawley watches Morphy opening the safe: "Joey dialed the mystic numbers and turned the wheel that drew the bolts. The holy of holies swung stately open and Mr. Baker took the salute of the assembled money" (Timmerman 260). On a less mundane but more traditional level, Hawley's own luck changes in *Winter* just as it does for

Arthur in the *Alliterative Morte*. Steinbeck invests the very moment in
which Hawley's fortune changes—when he receives the money from
Morphy—with the symbolism handed down by way of the Arthur myth,
thus enhancing the significance of the scene.

Like the other Arthurian novels of Steinbeck, *Winter* contains a
Grail story. Here the Grail symbol is the snake talisman that Ethan had
been given by his old Welsh aunt, Deborah. In the same way that, as
Dennis Prindle pointed out, a "Talismanic bond" holds the paisanos of
Tortilla Flat together (see Chapter II), this literal talisman forms a bond
in the Hawley family, particularly between Ethan and his daughter, Ellen,
with whom the talisman is associated most closely. The first time the talisman appears in the novel, for instance, is when Hawley sees the sleeping Ellen wearing it. Near the end of the novel, the talisman appears
again, significantly, in a scene where Hawley has just referred to his wife
by the pet name "my holy quail" (*Winter* 282). The use of the talisman
as a Grail object is not obvious, however, until the very end of the novel,
when Hawley, having betrayed his employer and friend for his own financial gain and having discovered that his moral degeneracy has spread to
his own son, who has cheated to win the "I Love America" essay contest, goes to the beach to slit his wrists. He is able to extricate himself
from his moral morass just by coming across the talisman/Grail in his
pocket, where Ellen has apparently placed it, knowing her father is feeling down. Once again, our Grail and its knight are somewhat unlikely
from an archetypal point of view. Hawley is a grocery store clerk who
deceives his boss and his best friend, among others, to come into a large
sum of money and change his fortune. We should note that no quest has
been required of Hawley to find this Grail. Instead, he happens upon it
completely by accident. Thus he is the most unlikely Grail knight that
Steinbeck ever produced. However, there is a deeper significance in Ellen
having placed the talisman in Hawley's pocket. Since she has competed
in the essay contest honestly, we may consider her to be the pure Grail
knight needed to achieve the Grail. And though she herself has no real
quest to speak of, she is able to deliver the Grail to the Fisher King of
this novel, who is Hawley himself.

What is particularly problematic here is not the lack of a Grail quest
in this novel, however, but rather the ease with which Hawley is apparently able to put his guilt aside by the mere finding of the talisman.
Howard Levant's summation of the novel's ending as a "*coup de theatre*,
a victory of plot over substance" (Levant 300) seems particularly apt.

As in *Sweet Thursday*, where the Grail's healing ability has been highly idealized, the ending of *Winter* suggests a similar simplicity in salvation — a simplicity notably absent from the Grail situations of the early Steinbeck works, wherein the Grail was found but always failed to deliver the Grail knight and the Fisher King from their predicaments. Even a bona fide criminal such as Hawley can be "saved."

What these endings seem to suggest is a growing idealism on Steinbeck's part. The earlier Steinbeck would perhaps have allowed Hawley to take his life, but the Steinbeck of *The Winter of Our Discontent* allows his villainous knight to live and even, perhaps, be truly changed by the talisman/Grail. As Michael J. Meyer comments on the talisman, it "has as much power as its owner endows it with. This is also similar to the Grail, which according to Arthurian legend, gains its power through faith." Meyer also notes the similarity in names between Ellen and the Arthurian Grail Mistress Elaine, "protector of the holy relic" (Meyer 265).

Why had Steinbeck's perspective on the Grail's redemptive power shifted so much? One factor may have been the Malory project. In the letter to Joseph Bryan, Steinbeck detailed his feelings about late 1950s America:

> [N]ext to our own time the 15th century was the most immoral time we know. Authority was gone. The church split, the monarchy without authority and manorial order disappearing [Steinbeck & Wallsten, 1989 649–50; Timmerman 257].

Despite this rather dismal outlook for the U.S., *Winter* actually offers a glimmer of hope, particularly in its ending, which is tied into the novel's own Grail symbolism. All these changes are consistent with the development of Steinbeck's view that the *Morte* could be seen as a guidebook for human conduct, particularly in a society where morality was decaying. Perhaps Steinbeck felt the situation in the late 1950s was more urgent than the Depression, but more likely he had simply grown tired of seeing the ideal promoted by the Arthurian legend defeated generation after generation by human nature. In response, he offered an example of the redemption available, unrealistic though it might be.

Steinbeck's view of American possibilities shifted yet again, however, with the election of John F. Kennedy to the presidency in 1960. In

this Steinbeck was no different from much of the country, from prominent celebrities like Frank Sinatra, who lent his vocal abilities to the
Kennedy campaign, to everyday citizens, young and old, who turned
out in droves to vote for the attractive and articulate war hero and candidate. Kennedy seemed to offer something substantially different from
previous candidates. For one thing, he was considerably younger than
his predecessor. (Kennedy would become the youngest American ever
elected to the presidency, while immediate predecessor Dwight Eisenhower was—until the election of Ronald Reagan in 1980—the oldest
man ever to ascend to America's highest office.) But beyond that, at the
close of the Eisenhower administration with its associated baggage (three
recessions, the rise and fall of Sen. Joseph McCarthy, the U-2 incident,
etc.), Americans were looking for *change*. This desire, perhaps more than
anything else, prompted Americans to opt for Kennedy over Eisenhower's vice president, Richard Nixon, though the margin of victory was
among the closest in American history, thanks in part to the divisive
issue of Kennedy's Roman Catholicism.

   None of these aspects of Kennedy's presidency were lost on Steinbeck, who outlived the president by five years. However, prior to
Kennedy's assassination in November 1963, Steinbeck was busy with
other projects. During the fall of 1960, which would have been the height
of the election campaign, Steinbeck was on the road with his pet poodle, Charley, writing down his thoughts and observations of a country
at the crossroads. While he encountered many of the social ills on this
journey that he'd written about for his whole career (the plight of workers, racism, etc.), he also reveled frequently in the beauty of the land
and the patchwork of people that he met who embodied what he felt was
best about America. These reflections were published in 1962 as *Travels
With Charley: In Search of America*. In the period between Steinbeck's
tour with Charley and the publication of *Travels*, Steinbeck was also
finishing up *The Winter of Our Discontent*. In the fall of 1962, Steinbeck
traveled to Stockholm to accept the Nobel Prize for Literature.

   Although it would not be until three years later that Steinbeck committed anything permanently to print regarding the Kennedy presidency,
assassination, and its legacy, he was not silent during that period. Before
Kennedy won the Democratic nomination, Steinbeck backed the twice-
defeated Democratic governor from Illinois, Adlai Stevenson, for the
nomination, going so far as to chair a New York–based exploratory committee on a third run for Stevenson (Benson *Writer* 877). Steinbeck and

Stevenson had a long-standing friendship dating back to the candidate's first run for the presidency in 1952. Steinbeck identified himself as a "Stevenson Democrat" and supported him with the enthusiasm that he had felt for Roosevelt three decades earlier. Steinbeck and Stevenson corresponded frequently until Stevenson's death in 1965, and Stevenson even visited Steinbeck while the author was at work on his Malory project. The politician mentioned his visit with Steinbeck in a December 1959 article in *Newsday* (Simmonds "Dream" 38-39).

Once Kennedy was nominated, Steinbeck kept quiet for the most part, though an interview he gave to the *San Francisco Chronicle* on the eve of the election offers an interesting juxtaposition of images that would be seen over and over again. The bulk of the interview involved Steinbeck's latest projects—mainly *The Winter of Our Discontent* and the Malory project, though passing reference is made to the writer's recent "travels" that would become *Travels with Charley*. The subject of the Malory project gave Steinbeck the opportunity to extemporize on the importance of Arthurian myth in American culture:

> "The American Western is the Arthurian cycle," [Steinbeck] observed. "The King is the man who solves everything with a gun. The Western has its Guinevere and Gawain, all the characters. Arthur did not originate in England; all people have their Arthur, and need him. He is created out of a need, when they are in trouble. *America's Arthur is coming* because the people need him" [Gentry 75, emphasis added].

"This did lead into politics," the interviewer, Curt Gentry, notes, and Steinbeck revealed that during his recent travels he had encountered voter enthusiasm that he had not seen in many years. Interestingly, the only candidate mentioned by name is Kennedy, and Gentry chose to title the interview with the emphasized text quoted above. The only reference to the impending election itself in *Travels* is a brief description by Steinbeck of his dread of facing his staunchly Republican sisters out in California and the relatively good-natured arguments over Kennedy versus Nixon that followed (*Travels* 199).

It should also be noted that while there is no sweeping Arthurian theme in *Travels with Charley*, a few explicit Arthurian references are made in the book that are characteristic of the author's work. On a very general level, Steinbeck casts *Travels* very much in the style of a quest by dubbing his trailer Rocinante, after Don Quixote's horse. More specifically, Steinbeck likens Deer Isle, Maine, to Avalon, the final resting place of Arthur according to Malory (*Travels* 52). Much later in the work, a meditation on the state of Texas leads Steinbeck to draw a comparison between what in many ways is America's most deeply mythic state and "those parts of England where King Arthur walked" (*Travels* 233). Finally, in a rather humorous observation in the redwood forests of California, Steinbeck remarks that the experience of his Long Island-raised poodle seeing the sequoias "might even be like that Galahad who saw the Grail" (*Travels* 188). The only difference, of course, being that Galahad most likely didn't view the Grail as a latrine.

Returning to politics, despite the absence of his explicit endorsement of Kennedy, Steinbeck was nonetheless invited to the inauguration of the new president on January 20, 1961. Steinbeck wrote a segment on the inauguration for inclusion in *Travels*, which was still in the editing stage in early 1961, but it was later cut. Steinbeck's only public comment regarding Kennedy's inaugural address — an obvious jab at Eisenhower — was to say that "Syntax ... [had] been restored to the highest place in the Republic" (Benson *Writer* 891-92). Steinbeck did send a short personal letter of thanks to the new president, remarking that "A nation may be moved by its statesmen and defended by its military but it is usually remembered for its artists. It does seem to me that you, sir, have discovered or rather rediscovered this lost truth" (Steinbeck and Wallsten, 1989 691). While Kennedy responded with a brief form letter bemoaning his inability that day to meet with Steinbeck and other artists and writers who were invited personally, he added a handwritten note on the page: "No President was ever prayed over with such fervor. Evidently they felt that the country or I needed it — probably both" (Steinbeck and Wallsten, 1989 691).

Thus began a personal relationship between Kennedy and Steinbeck that was further solidified when, in early 1963, the president nominated Steinbeck to be a sort of cultural ambassador to the Soviet Union and Eastern and Central Europe under the auspices of the United States Information Agency. After meeting the president several times and asking if he could take playwright Edward Albee (*Who's Afraid of Virginia Woolf?*) with him on the trip, it was decided that the two writers (and Steinbeck's wife Elaine) would embark on their cultural mission in October, traveling from Finland to the Soviet Union, and then to Poland, Hungary, Czechoslovakia, and West Berlin (Benson *Writer* 926). Because of this assignment given to him by Kennedy himself, Steinbeck was not even in the country on that fateful day in Dallas: On November 22, Steinbeck was in Warsaw when the news of the assassination flashed around the world. Steinbeck biographer Jackson Benson writes, "Their [Steinbeck and his wife] first instinct was to call home or to go home, but there was no way to get a call through, and after some thought, they decided they should continue the job that Kennedy had given them. They would attend the official meetings but cancel the social part of their schedule" (*Writer* 946).

Two days after the assassination, Steinbeck wrote letters from Warsaw to both Jacqueline Kennedy and the newly inaugurated president. In his letter to the slain president's widow, he recounted to her the outpouring of grief he saw among the Polish citizens. To President Johnson, he reiterated a pledge made to Jackie Kennedy — "Our hearts are with you." He also offered his support for the new president and stated his intention to continue the mission on which President Kennedy had sent him despite the tragedy. Finally, in the letter to Johnson, Steinbeck asked if Gov. John Connally of Texas might remember his wife, Elaine, who attended college with him at the University of Texas at Austin. (The editors of Steinbeck's letters note that Elaine Steinbeck knew not only Connally at Austin, but also Lady Bird Johnson.) In a response to Steinbeck, President Johnson thanked him for his support and wrote, "I am hopeful that very soon I may sit with you and talk about our country" (Steinbeck and Wallsten, 1989 787-88).

Steinbeck returned to the U.S. in early 1964 and met for the first of many times with Johnson. He also met Jackie Kennedy, who proposed to Steinbeck that he write an authorized biography of her husband. In response, Steinbeck sent Kennedy's widow a series of letters over the next few months as he tried to decide whether or not to accept the project. The first letter, dated February 25, 1964, expresses Steinbeck's fear that the project would too "huge and universal" to undertake, and that the mythic qualities of the fallen president would necessarily draw comparisons to past mythic heroes such as Buddha, Jesus, and, of course, Arthur (Steinbeck and Wallsten, 1989 793). In fact, Steinbeck refers specifically to Malory's *Morte* several times in the letter, noting, for instance, the similarity between the age of Malory and the present day (a theme John Gardner would take up in interviews regarding Malory's relevance to the twentieth-century reader) and even attaching a portion of the *Morte* to the letter — Sir Ector's lament over the corpse of Sir Launcelot (Steinbeck and Wallsten, 1989 791-92; 793). Eventually

Steinbeck turned down the project. As Steinbeck biographer Jackson Benson recounts, the "Kennedy approach to Arthur ... seemed to drift into limbo as he mulled [it] over in his mind" (*Writer* 951). In a final letter to Jackie Kennedy, Steinbeck wrote, "[O]ne day I do hope to write what we spoke of — how this man who was the best of his people, by his life and his death gave the best back to them for their own" (Steinbeck and Wallsten, 1989 800; Benson *Writer* 951). Such observations would also appear in Steinbeck's final work.

Steinbeck did embrace Kennedy's successor, Lyndon Johnson, with enthusiasm, helping to write the president's acceptance speech for the 1964 Democratic National Convention and then assisting in the writing of Johnson's January 1965 inaugural address ("America"). With passage of the Civil Rights Act of 1964 and the initiation of Johnson's "Great Society," the pessimism that Steinbeck felt in the aftermath of Kennedy's assassination was assuaged for a time (French "Steinbeck's" 10-11). In September 1964, Johnson awarded Steinbeck the United States Medal of Freedom (Kennedy had nominated Steinbeck for the medal), and afterwards, Steinbeck vocally supported Johnson on virtually every move the president made — including his escalation of the war in Vietnam. However, just as the activist presidency of Johnson was ruined by Vietnam, so eventually was Steinbeck's pessimism about the political process revived.

Steinbeck's support of the Vietnam War is baffling, considering his long-standing sympathies with left-wing politics and his having been labeled "red" back in the 1930s. In a 1965 letter to Jack Valenti, an assistant to Johnson, written soon after the death of Adlai Stevenson on July 14, Steinbeck said, "There is no way of making the Vietnamese war decent. There is no way of justifying sending troops to another man's country" (Steinbeck and Wallsten, 1989 826; Benson *Writer* 1018). However, Steinbeck's point of view changed, and, as Benson observes, Steinbeck "saw little connection between the totalitarianism of Communist Russia and the social programs of the New Deal in this country or the democratic socialism of countries in Europe. The Soviet Union, with its purges and political imprisonments, was far closer in his mind to Nazi Germany than to socialist Sweden" (*Writer* 967). Furthermore, Steinbeck's son, John Jr., was a combat soldier in Vietnam, and the resistance to the draft by sons of privilege similar to his own infuriated the writer (Benson *Writer* 970). Steinbeck became a sort of unofficial spokesman for the Vietnam cause, visiting the battle zone as a correspondent for *Newsday* and even exploiting his relationship with the Russian poet Yevgeny Yevtushenko (most famous for his poem "Babi Yar," on the Nazi execution of tens of thousands of Jews outside Kiev in 1941) for the cause of peace, suggesting that the influential poet could persuade his government to stop sending weapons to North Vietnam (Benson *Writer* 992-93).

Steinbeck's primary observations about the war concerned the American soldiers he saw fighting to "preserve democracy," and in this sense, he echoes his earlier statements in *Bombs Away* that America's soldiers and fighter pilots represent the best the United States has to offer. However, after perhaps too much time in the field and too much exposure to warfare more brutal than he had even seen during his time as a war correspondent in the European Theater of Operations during World War II, Steinbeck's unqualified support for the war began to diminish. In an August 1967 letter to editor Elizabeth Otis, as Benson notes, "[h]is reaction to the war had come almost full circle" (*Writer* 1018):

> I know we cannot win this war, nor any war for that matter. And it seems to me that the design is for us to sink deeper and deeper into it, more and more of us. When we have put down a firm foundation of our dead and when we have by a slow, losing process been sucked into the texture of Southeast Asia, we will never be able nor will we want to get out [Steinbeck and Wallsten, 1989 848; Benson *Writer* 1017].

The final straw was John Jr.'s arrest by the Army for possession of marijuana in October 1967, which brought to Steinbeck's full consciousness the extent of marijuana use among the combat soldiers in Vietnam. This essentially crushed Steinbeck's view that while the war itself was perhaps immoral, at least the men fighting it were of high moral character. By the end of the year, Steinbeck's support for the war was finished and there is no evidence of any further correspondence between Steinbeck and the president on the subject of the war — or anything else.

That same year, Steinbeck suffered from a ruptured disc in his back and remained hospitalized on and off for the rest of his life. While he was preparing for surgery in October 1967, Steinbeck gave an interview to Budd Schulberg in which he hinted that, despite his loss of confidence in Johnson and in the government in general, he still believed in the applicability of the Arthurian myth, even when it came to the ever-increasing number of hippies on the streets. Referring to medieval times, Steinbeck said:

[T]hose days are not so different from our own. An old order
was on the way out. Something new was in the air, but no
one knew exactly what lay ahead. The concept of chivalry
was essentially a humanistic idea — going forth to do good
deeds.... It's no accident that Kennedy's Court was also called
Camelot. But aside from the courtiers there were these individual knights roaming the land and searching for their own
individual values.... Maybe on the street corners today are
our own Galahads and Mordreds. But it needed an Arthur, a
Round Table, to hold them together [Simmonds "Dream"
31].

Clearly, the association between Kennedy and the Arthurian myth was
still strong in the writer's mind.

As noted above, Steinbeck's 1960 interview with the *San Francisco
Chronicle* juxtaposes the images of Kennedy and Arthur. It may be that
this is the first time this was done, though obviously it would not be the
last. The Kennedy-Camelot association would become one of the most
enduring applications of mythology to politics in American — and even
world — history. A series of curious links, including the *Chronicle* interview, seem to have built up this notion of Kennedy as an Arthur figure.
For one thing, less than a month after Kennedy's election to the presidency, Alan Jay Lerner and Frederick Loewe's musical *Camelot* premiered
on Broadway. Lerner and Loewe based the musical on British writer T.H.
White's *The Once and Future King*, a standard retelling of the Arthurian
tales. Musicologist William Everett writes:

Camelot came to represent much more than a popular entertainment based on the chivalrous era of King Arthur. In the
eyes of the public, its timely ascendancy corresponded to the
election and inauguration of John F. Kennedy. To many
Americans, among them the new president, both Arthur's
Camelot and the new administration represented an ideal
world — one filled with hope and dreams [Everett "Images"].

Everett goes on to suggest that portions of Kennedy's inaugural
address might have been culled from lines from the musical. For
instance, Everett draws two strong analogies using lines from Act I of
the musical: "This is the time of King Arthur, and we reach for the stars!
/ This is the time of King Arthur, and violence is not strength and com-
passion is not weakness" (Lerner 70). Everett then notes two intrigu-
ingly similar lines from Kennedy's inaugural address: First, Everett
evokes Kennedy's reference to putting a man on the moon before the

end of the decade and his specific suggestion, "Together, let us explore the stars"; second, in the context of his proposal to form the Peace Corps, Everett reminds us that Kennedy stated, "So let us begin anew — remembering on both sides that civility is not a sign of weakness" (Kennedy 307). Clearly Everett is suggesting that Lerner and Loewe's musical was a primary source for the inaugural address (Everett "Images"). Lerner and Kennedy were classmates and friends at the prestigious Choate school and later undergraduates at Harvard together, and this personal link may have inspired Kennedy to borrow from Lerner in his address.

It has been stated repeatedly that Kennedy was a fan of the musical and would sing portions of it to himself in his less guarded moments. The greatest perpetuator of this image of Kennedy was the president's widow, who told *Life* reporter and family friend Theodore White of the president's fondness for the musical not long after the assassination. As White would later recall, Jackie Kennedy called him to Hyannis Port to tell him that she wanted the Camelot theme to be the enduring legacy of her husband's administration. "At night before we'd go to sleep," the first lady told White, "Jack liked to play some records ... and the song he loved most came at the very end of this record, the last side of *Camelot*, sad *Camelot*: 'Don't let it be forgot, that once there was a spot, for one brief shining moment that was known as Camelot.'" (Klein "Human"). White committed the first lady's words to print, and the legacy was sealed.

It has been debated by historians just how much of Kennedy's purported love of the musical was actually true and how much was manufactured after the president's death by his widow; but no one can deny that the mythic aspects of Kennedy — with or without the Camelot trappings — remain, though the Arthurian aspect of the myth continues to appear in analyses of the president. For instance, historian Thomas Brown succinctly states some negative aspects of the link between the Arthurian myth and the Kennedy administration:

> It is possible to find deep latent meanings in Camelot. The image is especially interesting because the United States was conceived in the revolt of a simple, virtuous 'Country' against the decadence and grandeur of the English 'Court.' Camelot, then, may be taken as a metaphor for how the New Frontiersmen conceived of themselves.... The use of a monarchical symbol to describe the government of a republic can be seen as the natural outcome of Kennedy's tendency toward

> centralized, personalized authority based on 'charisma'....
> But in the end, the Camelot image seems more banal and
> fake than dangerous.... It is only appropriate, then, that it was
> not inspired by the genuine legend ... but by the insipidly
> sentimentalized version in a Broadway musical [*JFK* 42-43].

Clearly Brown belongs to the school of presidential historians who view Kennedy from a standpoint more negative than positive. However, it should be noted that many who evoked the Camelot metaphor posthumously for Kennedy were not historians— including John Steinbeck.

Steinbeck lived just long enough to see Johnson walk away from the presidency and Richard Nixon narrowly defeat Vice President Hubert Humphrey in the 1968 election before dying on December 20 of that year. Steinbeck did not pass away, however, without leaving *America and Americans*, his final written work, which was published in 1966. Viking had approached Steinbeck in 1964 and asked him to write a series of captions for a photo essay on America that they planned to publish. The captions evolved into essays, and much of the material that Steinbeck had excised from *Travels with Charley* appeared in this last work. *America and Americans* presents the author's homeland, warts and all: "complicated, paradoxical, bullheaded, shy, cruel, boisterous, unspeakably dear, and very beautiful" (*America* 9). The various essays often bear no relationship to the montage of photographs that they accompany (among the photographers whose work appeared in the volume was celebrated photographer Alfred Eisenstaedt, whose contributions included a photograph of a drunken parade marcher and a snapshot of a girl scout in front of a statue of Abraham Lincoln), but they contain many of the themes that Steinbeck had been developing over his entire career.

For instance, the Arthurian cycle of mythology is still on Steinbeck's mind in *America and Americans,* and the author expands on a theme he stated in the *San Francisco Chronicle* interview six years earlier:

> The dreams of a people either create folk literature or find
> their way into it; and folk literature, again, is always based
> on something that happened. Our most persistent folk tales—
> constantly retold in books, movies, and television shows—
> concern cowboys, gunslinging sheriffs, and Indian fighters....
> [T]he brave and honest sheriff who with courage and six-gun
> brings law and order and civic virtue to a Western commu-
> nity is perhaps our most familiar hero, no doubt descended
> from the brave mailed knight of chivalry who battled and

overcame even with lance and sword ... I think that surviving folk tales are directly based on memory. There must have
been a leader like King Arthur; although there is no historical record to prove it, the very strength of the story presumes
his existence [*America* 40].

Later in the work, Steinbeck considers Americans' obsession with
societies and orders steeped in medievalism, writing that "[a]long with
veterans' organizations, Americans have developed scores of orders
lodges and encampments ... Knights Templar, Woodmen of the World,
Redmen ... the *World Almanac* lists hundreds of such societies" (*America*
89-90). It is probably no accident that in his listing of fraternal orders,
Steinbeck includes the Knights Templar, considering their aforementioned mythological connection to the Holy Grail and the inclusion of
imagery of the Masonic order in *The Winter of Our Discontent*.

Throughout *America and Americans*, Steinbeck touches on the
political process, both in general and specifically. For instance, in one
passage, Steinbeck expounds on the relationship between Americans and
their chief executive:

The relationship of Americans to their President is a matter
of amazement to foreigners. Of course we respect the office
and admire the man who can fill it, but at the same time we
inherently fear and suspect power.... We insist that the
President be cautious in speech, guarded in action, immac-
ulate in his public and private life; and in spite of these
imposed pressures we are avidly curious about the man hid-
den behind the formal public image we have created.... And
with all this, Americans have a love for the President that
goes beyond loyalty or party nationality; he is ours, and we
exercise the right to destroy him [*America* 47-48].

Because there is no chronological or other specific order to the essays in
the work, political references run throughout *America and Americans*,
and while these references cannot be said to become progressively more
specific, there are political passages that are clearly more specific than
this rather vague reflection on the love-hate relationship that Americans
have with the presidency.

There seem, for example, to be references to both Kennedy and
Nixon in Steinbeck's observation that Americans "will vote against a
man because of his religion [Kennedy], his name, or the shape of his nose
[Nixon]" (*America* 34). In further considering the relationship between

the citizens and the president, Steinbeck gets more specific (and more personal):

> In President Roosevelt's third and fourth terms, many people who had been his passionate partisans were turned against him by pure uneasiness over the perpetuation of power. On the crest of this feeling it was easy to put through a law limiting the Presidency to two terms—a law which soon after embarrassed its Republican proponents, who would have liked to keep President Eisenhower in office indefinitely [*America* 44].

But it is President Kennedy to whom Steinbeck refers most directly and most poignantly.

Steinbeck was perhaps inspired to meditate most deeply on Kennedy not only because of the relative proximity of the assassination to the composition of *America and Americans* and Jackie Kennedy's request that he write a biography of JFK, but also because of one of the photographs Viking selected to include in the volume: A 1960 photo of Kennedy and Johnson on the campaign trail that appears as a two-page spread on pages 64 and 65 of the book. (The photograph was taken by Jacques Lowe, a friend of the Kennedy family who became the unofficial White House photographer during Kennedy's tenure as president. A collection of his photographs from the Kennedy Administration was published in 1996 as the evocatively titled *Camelot: The Kennedy Years*.) "It is my firm belief," Steinbeck writes, "that President Kennedy was murdered not for what he was but for what his murderer wasn't: a man with a beautiful and loving wife, a high position, and the respect and admiration of his countrymen could not be forgiven by a man who had failed in everything he had undertaken" (*America* 91). Apparently Steinbeck took the findings of the Warren Commission at face value, and elsewhere he says, presumably of Lee Harvey Oswald, "I do not know anyone who does not feel a little guilty that out of our soil the warped thing grew that could kill him [Kennedy]" (*America* 48).

Here Steinbeck's sentiments mirror almost identically Thomas Brown's observations of how the Camelot myth came into play in the aftermath of the assassination and in several years to follow. Brown writes, "From the perspective of those creating this image [the image of the Kennedy administration as Camelot], the Kennedy assassination had almost totemic significance: it was the sacrificial offering of the prince of Camelot to the forces of bigotry, irrationalism, and fanaticism" (*JFK*

104). For Brown, Kennedy's Camelot offers a united front against the forces of evil: "Camelot, like any symbol, served to congeal diverse ideas and emotions in a single image.... While RFK contemplated whether he should oppose LBJ in 1968, an admirer in Evanston, Illinois, wrote: 'Please reconvene the round table. We want Camelot again'" (*JFK* 42). The "monarchical" aspects of both Camelot and the Kennedy dynasty noted by Brown are underscored by the notion that Robert Kennedy would be a suitable leader based on his pedigree alone.

Insofar as Steinbeck, in the *Chronicle* interview and certainly in his letters to Jackie Kennedy and conversation with Budd Schulberg, was a part of the myth's perpetuation (if not its creation), Brown's analysis of the assassination and its mythic significance seems to speak almost directly to Steinbeck's assessment of Oswald as the embodiment of everything wrong with America. Unfortunately for the author, his acceptance of not only the Warren Commission's findings but his baffling allegiance to Johnson's Vietnam policy until his personal life was affected by it seems to suggest that, near the end of his life, unlike in the 1930s, Steinbeck was not in the best shape to judge what was truly wrong with his country. Other writers who began their careers and flourished in this period when Steinbeck was in twilight might better exemplify how Arthurian literature by Americans reflected the effects of this tumultuous period.

CHAPTER VI

John Gardner

John Gardner spent the early years of his career as a scholar in the field of medieval studies, so it is no wonder that his fiction has a strong medieval flavor. Among Gardner's scholarly works are *The Complete Works of the Gawain-Poet*, translations of several Middle English poems including the *Alliterative Morte Arthure*, and *Cliff's Notes* on *Le Morte d'Arthur* and the works of the Gawain-Poet. With such a strong emphasis on Arthurian works in his scholarly writing, it is perhaps surprising that Gardner never wrote an Arthurian novel on the level of Twain's *Connecticut Yankee*, Steinbeck's *Tortilla Flat*, or even Chandler's *The Big Sleep*. Instead, Gardner offered as his medievalist fiction the *Beowulf* story told from the point of view of the monster (*Grendel*), the consolidation of power by a sixteenth-century Swedish king (*Freddy's Book*), and several short works found in the collection *The King's Indian*. Nevertheless, Arthurian literature, and in particular Malory's *Morte*, were never far from Gardner's mind, and a careful look at a few of his novels will show a writer who, like Twain, Steinbeck, and Chandler, used Arthurian symbolism and imagery to comment on modern America's social problems.

Gardner felt very strongly that one of art's (and thus fiction's) primary purposes was to instruct, and thus he set out in his 1978 volume *On Moral Fiction* to delineate how fiction can prescribe moral attitudes and action. A representative excerpt serves as an example:

> In a democratic society, where every individual opinion counts, and where nothing, finally, is left to some king or group of party elitists, art's incomparable ability to instruct, to make alternatives intellectually and emotionally clear, to spotlight falsehood, insincerity, foolishness — art's incomparable ability, that is, to make us understand — ought to be a

> force bringing people together, breaking down barriers of
> prejudice and ignorance, and holding up ideals worth pur-
> suing [*Moral* 42].

Unfortunately, Gardner also frequently attacked his contemporaries for
not writing moral fiction — particularly postmodernists like Pynchon
and William Gass— and this earned him some enemies on the critical
front (though he managed to make a friend of Gass).

Notably, Gardner did not list Malory among the authors who he
believed created moral fiction, though he did state once in an interview,
echoing Steinbeck's belief, "I think the book to buy a boy is Malory's
Morte d'Arthur so that he'll know he's supposed to be a knight" (Natov
and DeLuca 99). Gardner found the *Morte* to be a fascinating work not
just because of its content, but because of its form, its author, and its
time. For instance, Gardner saw the Middle Ages as a major turning
point in history and Malory as playing a key role in these changes:

> The Middle Ages was the end of a different civilization.
> Someplace in the sixteenth century the Middle Ages stopped.
> In the fifteenth and sixteenth century all the genres break
> down. It becomes impossible to write a straight romance, or
> a straight anything. And everybody who is anybody starts
> form-jumping ... and Malory comes out with *Morte d'Arthur*,
> which is a freaky new kind of form, a breakdown of all kinds
> of other forms [Bellamy and Ensworth 9].

In another interview, Gardner said of Malory's time, "Things were
reduced to a situation in which the church was the only educated body;
a Hitler-like fiend was on the throne in Henry IV; every decent mind in
the country, like Thomas Malory, was in prison" (Reilly 79).

Gardner was able to make Malory's work relevant to a twentieth-
century audience mainly by suggesting that we are at a similar crossroads in modern times. John Howell writes that Gardner "saw Malory's
vision as dark and despairing, and totally compatible with that of the
twentieth century" (*Understanding* 42). Elsewhere, Gardner stated
explicitly what Howell implies. "Right now," he once said, "all of society is where Chaucer and Malory were: staring at the abyss. In 14th and
15th-century literature there is nothing but one long gasp of despair ...
Malory's *Morte d'Arthur* is the most 20th-century book you'll ever read"
(Diehl 3). Even to his youngest readers he delivered this message, writing in the *Cliff's Notes* on Malory, "Malory's grim vision has relevance

for any kingdom or civilization: the very forces which make civilization necessary must in the end, if Malory is right, bring it to ruin" (*Notes* 5).

There is one final way in which Malory's work finds expression through Gardner's fiction. Gardner employs the medieval rhetorical device of *inventio*, which he has defined as "the collection of old materials to be used in a new way." Per Winther notes that the Gawain-poet employed this method as part of his collage technique (*Art* 90); so did Malory, and Gardner published scholarly works on both writers, as we have already seen. Gardner's use of the *inventio* technique is apparent in all of his major works: In *Grendel*, for instance, the "old material" is *Beowulf*; in *The Sunlight Dialogues*, the old material is primarily ancient Babylonian and Hebrew mythology; and in *October Light*, there seems to be a deliberate use of the old-woman-in-the-attic genre of gothic fiction, though with the many twists that Gardner adds, it is barely recognizable as such.

Gardner's first novel, *The Resurrection*, uses *inventio* in its integration of the philosophy of R.G. Collingwood into the text. The use of this material imparts an overly philosophical tone, and the novel is unfortunately among the least of Gardner's accomplishments. *The Resurrection* contains almost no Arthurian imagery at all. The novel tells the tale of James Chandler's discovery that he has only weeks to live because of leukemia. Chandler has been a professor of philosophy at a San Francisco Bay Area university, but he makes the decision to return with his wife and three young daughters to his boyhood home (and Gardner's boyhood home) of Batavia, New York, to spend his final days. While Chandler is in Batavia waiting to die, he has some final ruminations on death and some interactions with figures from his childhood. There is little here to suggest an Arthurian subtext at work. However, during several dream sequences that form a crucial part of the novel, an image familiar to readers of Arthurian literature — the Wheel of Fortune — seems to appear.

Gardner tells us that "invariably [Chandler] saw himself in his dreams as heroic" (*Resurrection* 38). However, once his awareness of his own mortality takes on a new poignancy, Chandler's dreams become frightening. One of the very first of these dreams finds the philosopher in a junk shop, and he happens upon a modern representation of a familiar medieval symbol:

> He was listening to the unearthly music and looking at something, a small, rusty gear — a wheel — suspended, supported by nothing but air, three inches from the floor. Chandler real-

ized all at once that all the queer machines were running and
the tiny wheel was turning, spinning at incredible speed,
shooting off terrible sparks of brilliant color — yellow, green,
blueish red [*Resurrection* 23].

Several chapters later, the symbol recurs in another dream:

In what seemed like the center, in a kind of chamber framed
by what looked like the disintegrating remains of an intri-
cately carved rosewood clock, there stood, or rather hung,
supported by nothing, a wheel .... He put on his glasses and
studied the turns of the wheel with care, smiling and nod-
ding at each full revolution, and counting: *One, one, one ....*
This time the wheel turned on and on, faster and faster, by
some law of its own, and the rumbling sound was louder and
closer, and he knew that it was the clatter of things in motion
[*Resurrection* 128].

That Gardner finds it necessary to repeat the image of the spinning wheel
draws additional attention to the symbol.

It was a symbol that Gardner had very much in mind during the
1960s and early 1970s, when he was composing not only *The Resurrection*,
but also *The Sunlight Dialogues*. (By a contractual arrangement, *Sunlight
Dialogues* was released after *Grendel*, though it was written earlier. *The
Wreckage of Agathon* was also published in the interim.) Further, Gardner
was translating several anonymous Middle English poems, among them
the *Alliterative Morte Arthure*, which has the Wheel of Fortune as a pivotal image:

And she whirled a wheel around with her two white hands,
And she turned that wheel as deftly as ever she pleased.
The rim was of yellow gold, with royal stones
Array in wonderful wealth, and rubies aplenty;
The spokes of the wheel were resplendent with splinters of
silver
Springing out, all dazzling, the space of a spear-length
[*Alliterative* 3260-66].

The image of the wheel from the medieval prototype bears some resemblance to its appearance in *The Resurrection*, particularly in the use of
color imagery alongside the wheel's symbolism. Just as the Wheel of
Fortune in the *Alliterative Morte* foretells Arthur's fall from power, the
wheels in James Chandler's dreams symbolize his own mortal fall.

Given its time of composition, it is not surprising that the idea of fortune, minus the wheel, turns up in *The Sunlight Dialogues*. Gardner uses the epigrams that precede several of the chapters of the novel to hint at the importance of the concept of fortune to the work. For example, the epigram preceding Chapter II — "His diademe of dyamans droppede adoun; / His weyes were a-wayard wroliche wrout; / Tynt was his tresor, tour, & toun" (Gardner *Sunlight* 63) — is attributed to an anonymous fourteenth-century source. These lines bear a strong resemblance to two lines from the *Alliterative Morte*: "His diadem had fallen, adorned with stones, / All indented with diamonds, designed for the time" (3295-96). These lines appear in the Wheel of Fortune scene of the poem and refer to one of the kings who, like Arthur, is tied to the wheel and is subject to its motions.

The epigram preceding Chapter III is less cryptic and is drawn from Malory: "But fortune ys so varyaunte, and the wheele so mutable, that there ys no constaunte abydyng. And that may be preved by many olde cronycles …" (*Sunlight* 135). Here the character decrying fortune's turn is Sir Launcelot, who says these lines as he bids adieu to Camelot before Arthur and Gawain prepare to make war against him for having killed Gawain's brothers. The major change between the anonymous poem and Malory is that in the *Alliterative Morte*, it is Arthur who finds himself bound to the wheel and set to fall, while in Malory's *Morte*, Launcelot is the victim of fortune who evokes the image of the wheel. (Obviously, Arthur too suffers at the hands of fortune, but the use of the symbolism of the Wheel of Fortune remains Launcelot's domain in Malory.) The man bound to the Wheel of Fortune in *The Sunlight Dialogues* is Police Chief Fred Clumly, who is locked in a battle of wills with the Sunlight Man — an initially anonymous drifter who has come to Batavia, where Clumly lives and works, and has spray-painted the word "love" on the sidewalk. The Sunlight Man breaks out of the jail and then challenges Clumly intellectually in a series of four dialogues that take place throughout the novel.

There are essentially two ways of looking at how Gardner introduces Arthurian elements into *The Sunlight Dialogues*. One is rather obvious, while the other has required remarks from Gardner to clarify it. First, we may regard Clumly as an Arthur figure. Winther offers some evidence for this point of view (though he is the major proponent of the other). He writes that the broad cast of characters in *The Sunlight Dialogues* resembles the *Morte* in the "need to put ideational and emotional pressures on the central character, Clumly" (*Art* 59). Elsewhere, he elaborates:

> The Maloryan echoes serve several purposes in the novel. For one thing, they lend a touch of Camelot to the Police Chief's law-and-order efforts, revealing an inability on Clumly's part to bend and adjust old-fashioned value judgments to new times. A good medieval knight was inherently loyal to the established codes of chivalry; Clumly likewise blindly accepts for a long time the rightness of law books [Winther *Art* 179].

David Cowart concurs in a similar analysis:

> The Malory influence ... moves the narrator to give his story something of the air of medieval romance, with the police as knights errant, Chief Clumly as their beleaguered king, and the Sunlight Man as the magician or enchanter they must do battle with. Malory is also behind the pervasive sense of loss and decline in the novel — the infinite sadness attending the order that has passed ... [Cowart 61].

The role that Clumly plays in the first Arthurian paradigm is that of Arthur. He makes this clear when he tells Kozlowski, "You're forgetting something. I'm responsible for this town, you follow that? Responsible! It's like a king. I don't mean I'm comparing myself to a king, you understand, but it's *like* a king. If a king's laws get tangled up and his knights all fail him, he's got to do the job himself. They're *his* people" (*Sunlight* 415).

Once we establish Clumly as an Arthur figure, it is not difficult to see the characters surrounding him as fulfilling other roles from the Arthurian tales. Howell, for instance, paints Arthur Hodge Sr. as a Fisher King (*Understanding* 46) and Millie Hodge as Morgan le Fay (50). Winther suggests that the Old Judge who appears at the beginning of the novel can be seen as a Merlin figure, although, Winther qualifies, he has "evidently forfeited a wisdom he once possessed" (Winther 97). Cowart again agrees: "[The Judge] invites anagogic interpretation as a kind of degenerate deity, a once-powerful god reduced to making feeble boasts ..." (Cowart 57). In this sense, the judge is not unlike Merlin, who in the *Morte* forfeited his own wisdom for the love of Nimue. In the very first scene of the novel, the judge himself seems to be aware of the association and relishes it: "'Take any ordinary man, give him a weapon — say, x caliber —' (he chuckled wickedly)" (*Sunlight* 1).

The other — and perhaps richer — way of looking at the Arthurian structure behind *The Sunlight Dialogues* is to consider the entire novel as a dialectic between Dante and Malory, an approach suggested by the author himself. "Healthy fiction is dialectic: the writer's understanding increases with each book he solves," Gardner wrote in *On Moral Fiction* (198). In an oft-cited interview, Gardner explained how two very disparate works — *Le Morte d'Arthur* and *The Divine Comedy* — were at work when he was composing the novel:

> [T]hough I don't mention it in the novel, Chief Fred Clumly in *Sunlight* once read Dante on a ship, though he no longer remembers it. It sank deep into the swamp of his mind and now throws strange light on his modern-seeming problems. The narrator of the novel has obviously read and pondered hard on Malory's *Morte d'Arthur*, which presents a medieval world view totally opposed to Dante's [Ferguson et al. 162].

In this dialectic, Clumly represents not Malory but Dante and the Italian poet's sense of order — in particular *law* and order. Gardner wrote in his prospectus of the novel for his publisher, "In contrast to those who dismiss or renounce order, asserting the flight to freedom … are those who, like Clumly, are mainly concerned with enforcing law and order" (Gardner "Plan" 273). Conveniently, since Clumly is the chief of police, he is readily identifiable in the law-and-order role, both to the reader and to Taggert Hodge, the Sunlight Man, who represents the chaos that distinguishes Malory's work. "The message of *Le Morte Darthur* [sic]," writes Winther, "is exactly the opposite [of Dante's], pointing to a *lack* of order as witnessed by the social upheavals that it describes" (*Art* 179)

Winther has written extensively on how the dialectic between Clumly/Dante and Sunlight/Malory works in the novel. Clumly begins the novel as a proponent of law and order, and his primary objective in regard to the Sunlight Man is to capture him for his crimes. The relationship of such a characterization to Dante — particularly the Dante of *The Divine Comedy* — rests on Dante's view of justice being doled out in Hell, Purgatory, and Heaven, with each realm having its own innate order and discipline. Cowart suggests that Clumly's blind wife Esther acts as an analogue to Dante's Beatrice, who leads the poet after he parts ways with Vergil (Cowart 62). The couple's initial alienation from anything regarding the disorder of Malory's universe is implied in a reference Gardner makes to Esther having "read to [Clumly] from a book in braille about Sir Lancelot, some story of adventure and romance so touching and foreign to them both that it made them blush and stop the reading for a while from embarrassment and fear" (*Sunlight* 11).

Taggert Hodge's association with the Arthurian realm is more difficult to identify. Drawing back a bit to his genealogy, we see that his father was Arthur Hodge Sr., a congressman. In the Hodge family, we see a house in disarray partly because of an ineffectual patriarch. This situation recalls not only the Fisher King scenario, but the *Morte*— particularly because the patriarch in question is named Arthur. The role Taggert seems to play in this scenario is that of Merlin. Howell posits that Gardner "employed the romance as a controlling metaphor, introducing an Arthur figure and a Merlin figure; and setting scenes in a castlelike police station, a basement which resembles a dungeon, a Gothic-style church, and a burial crypt" (*Understanding* 42). In Howell's analysis, this Merlin figure is Taggert Hodge.

"The Sunlight Man," Winther writes, "as a fictional character fits nicely into the context of medieval romance, a magician of hardly less formidable powers than Malory's Merlin" (*Art* 181). Gregory Morris's analysis is perhaps the most succinct: "[The Sunlight Man] enters, out of nowhere, nameless, as the 'official wizard to the king,' Clumly's interesting, if unsolicited, advisor. Hodge is magician and priest and diviner; his purpose is to bring Clumly closer to the proper state of divine kingship and to illuminate the dark spots in Clumly's world" (Morris "Babylonian" 34).

The Sunlight Man also fits the Merlin role as other American writers of Arthuriana have fleshed it out. By embracing the concept of "love" that he spray-paints on the pavement — at least ostensibly — and by appearing in the novel in hippie attire, Taggert Hodge is consistently drawn as a figure closer to nature than the other characters around him. In this way, he resembles both the Merlin of the Aeolian harp that we saw in Emerson's poetry and the Merlin of Cannery Row that Steinbeck created with his characterization of Doc in *Cannery Row*. Even the characterization of Hodge as a man on the margins of society has some basis in the Merlin mythos. In the medieval cycle of Merlin plays that depict the magician as being mad; in *The Sunlight Dialogues*, Hodge's behavior and the rambling nature of the dialogues imply the mind of a madman at work.

The four dialogues in which Hodge and Clumly engage are not at all Arthurian in scope or content. Rather, Hodge lectures Clumly on the virtues of ancient Babylonian civilization over ancient Hebrew civilization. The underlying themes of the lectures, however, are in keeping with the dialectic on which the characters are based. The ancient Babylonians embraced chaos, while the ancient Hebrews loved order. More importantly, Hodge touches on two subjects of important social and cultural value in the dialogues. The first dialogue is called the Dialogue of Wood and Stone because it deals with the idols of the religion of the Babylonians. In this dialogue, Hodge tells Clumly, "I was in CORE [the Congress of Racial Equality] in San Francisco when they decided to segregate it" (*Sunlight* 353). This reference is significant for two reasons: It introduces the theme of civil rights—a subject that would have been getting much press during the novel's composition period—and it leads into a criticism of an attempt to impose order on something that by definition should not have such an order, i.e., the racial segregation of a civil-rights group. Hodge is stating that by imposing order on the organization, the organization—and thus the ideals for which the organization was working—was ruined.

The second dialogue between Clumly and the Sunlight Man, dubbed the Dialogue of Houses, is a dissertation by Hodge on astrology—a pseudoscience that comes our way via the Babylonians. The "houses" of the dialogue's title refer to the houses of the zodiac. Once again, comparisons are made between ancient Babylon and ancient Israel. During the dialogue, Hodge makes a surprising remark:

> [T]he sexual revolution is a step in the wrong direction—an anti-puritanism which has only disastrous results. For one thing, a loss of mystery, and heightened guilt of a new, strictly psychological kind ... But it remains a possibility that the wrong step, the sexual revolution, might yet be transformed by accident of history to a mediate step toward a right step. The revolution leads away from ancient Israel. It does not lead home to Babylon, but it may make Babylon once again a live option [*Sunlight* 465].

Here Hodge makes the dialectic at work between Hebrew and Babylonian plain. He also hints at a view of the sexual revolution that Gardner explored in greater detail in *October Light*.

The third dialogue is dubbed the Dialogue of the Dead, so-called because in it Hodge discusses the Babylonian epic *Gilgamesh* with Clumly and specifically the flood narrative it contains that is the forerunner of the Biblical tale of Noah. During this dialogue, the Sunlight Man makes reference to John F. Kennedy, pointing out that just as every little girl wants to be Marie Curie, "the inventor of radium," every little boy wants to grow up to be the president of the United States. However, both examples are tainted. Marie Curie died of cancer because of her studies with radioactive substances, and Kennedy was assassinated. It is this latter example that is most significant for our discussion, since it was the Kennedy White House that came to be known in the collective consciousness of the country as "Camelot." Along with Vietnam, the assassination of Kennedy was one of the historical events that gave rise to the counterculture of the Sixties and a general distrust of government and authority that the Sunlight Man represents here. Had the *The Sunlight Dialogues* been composed after 1974, Watergate would no doubt be included in the list of grievances.

In the final dialogue, the Dialogue of Towers, which concerns the towers (like Babel) that the Babylonians built, the Sunlight Man offers Clumly this prophecy: "The capitalistic basis of the great values of Western culture will preclude solution of the world's problems. Vietnam is the beginning. No matter how long it takes, the end is upon us, not only in the East, but in Africa too, and in South America." This is Hodge's second reference to Vietnam, the first coming during the Dialogue of Houses, wherein he recalls a student of his being called before the House Un-American Activities Committee for his anti-war activities (*Sunlight* 468). It is important to note that the Vietnam War was escalating when Gardner was writing *The Sunlight Dialogues*, and putting this reference to the conflict in Taggert Hodge's mouth is another citation of the political and societal ills that the U.S. was facing during that period. Hodge sees "total chaos" enveloping the "political sphere," and his prediction is without a doubt true: One need only recall the social and cultural strife of the mid- to late 1960s. Hodge seals the prophecy with a nice medievalist flourish: "I give you my word as an official wizard to the king" (*Sunlight* 698).

The expectation of any dialectic is that the pre-existing thesis and antithesis will give rise to a new synthesis. In an interview, Gardner tried to explain how synthesis arises in *The Sunlight Dialogues* by stating, "[Y]ou have to cling to your rituals, yet develop a powerful sense of empathy for other people through particular relationships with other people (Natov and DeLuca 125). As Winther puts it, "Gardner's ideas are of no interest unless they are placed in a human context, be it private, social, or political" (*Art* 150). The synthesis that arises from the dialectic interaction of thesis (law and order) and antithesis (chaos) is justice. Morris writes, "Clumly takes a bit of the Babylonian and mixes it with a bit of the Arthurian and a bit of the Hebraic, and emerges with an interesting image of the benign, responsible leader" (Morris *Order* 81). Further, he learns "that the law, paradoxically, must sometimes be ignored in the service of justice" (Morris *Order* 83). Most critics point to Clumly's speech before the Dairy League—a speech that ends up turning into a eulogy for the Sunlight Man—as a recognition of these truths. As Leonard Butts concludes, it is Clumly "[trying] for the first time to put into words what he has learned" (Butts 83).

After publishing *The Sunlight Dialogues*, Gardner released in 1973 two works: his epic poem *Jason and Medeia*; and the pastoral novel *Nickel Mountain*, the latter of which, like *The Sunlight Dialogues*, had been written long before it appeared in print. The following year saw the publication of *The King's Indian: Stories and Tales*, and then in 1976 came *October Light*. This novel's publication in the Bicentennial year was no accident: Gardner intended the novel to be a commentary on the state of the nation at that time. "*October Light*," Morris writes, "by necessity, had to be published in 1976, for its subject is America—its present spiritual condition, and its likely direction in the future" (Morris *Order* 143). In this vein, there are epigrams from several of the founding fathers—among them Benjamin Franklin, John Adams, and George Washington—preceding the novel's chapters, in much the same way that epigrams set the tone in *The Sunlight Dialogues*. Similarly, the fellow Vermont native Ethan Allen is frequently in the thoughts of the characters of *October Light*, more often for his enigmatic ideas about freedom of the individual within a democracy and his tendency to drunkenness than for his wisdom. Ethan Allen is the same figure Steinbeck concentrates on in his novel about the state of the union, *The Winter of Our Discontent* (see Chapter V).

October Light concerns the ongoing battle between Vermont farmer James Page and his sister Sally, who are polar opposites in their points of view regarding feminism, civil rights, and just about everything else. In a violent rage one day, James destroys Sally's television with his shotgun and confines Sally to an upstairs room, where she comes across a pulp novel, *The Smugglers of Lost Souls' Rock*, which she reads and which Gardner includes in the text proper of the novel in extended excerpts. *Smugglers* is important to our study because it contains the one Arthurian reference in all of *October Light*. Peter Wagner, the protagonist of *Smugglers*, finds himself aboard the ship *New Jerusalem* after an attempt to kill himself by jumping from a bridge. The ship's skipper, Captain Fist, introduces Wagner to the rest of the crew, including the young woman who has resuscitated him:

> The Captain chuckled wickedly. "And Jane here —" he began. He paused, seemingly at a loss, and leaned forward until his snaky eyes emerged from the murky smoke. "What was Guinevere to King Arthur's court, or the Virgin Mary to the Christian religion? The coronet! The jewel that gives it all meaning!" He laughed till he coughed [*October* 98].

The Captain's remarks are highly ironic — particularly his juxtaposition of the Virgin Mary with Guinevere. After all, Guinevere may have been the Queen of Camelot, but she was also a fallen woman in the sense that her adultery with Launcelot was known, even to King Arthur himself. Further, Jane is a proponent of free love and engages in sexual relations with all the crew members and entourage of the *New Jerusalem*. Thus, to compare Jane to Guinevere is a debasement of the Arthurian legend, because even Guinevere's adultery was limited to Launcelot and based not on sex *per se* but on love. Even the name of the ship — the *New Jerusalem* — is ironic in that instead of alluding to the New Jerusalem of the New Testament in which the faithful would live free from sin after the Second Coming, this ship is smuggling marijuana.

One other character from *The Smugglers of Lost Souls' Rock* perhaps has a precedent in Arthurian literature, and this is Dr. Alkahest's housekeeper Pearl. We should recall that this name would have some significance for Gardner, who translated a poem by the title of *Pearl* when translating the complete works of the Gawain-poet. However, there are distinct differences: The Pearl of the medieval poem is the deceased daughter of the poet, while the Pearl of *Smugglers* is a middle-aged black woman harassed by the police for her efforts to locate a Dr. Alkahest. However, Gardner titles Chapter 12 of *Smugglers* "The Price of Pearl," recalling Steinbeck's dubbing of the pearl of his novella of the same name as "the pearl of great price." Steinbeck himself was relying on the medieval poem's model when he wrote *The Pearl*, and it is a fair assumption that, at the very least, Gardner relied on Steinbeck in titling this chapter. Also, a tangential relationship exists between the character of Pearl and the Arthurian poem *Sir Gawain and the Green Knight* by virtue of the two medieval poems sharing the same putative author.

In *On Moral Fiction*, Gardner delineated his underlying philosophical plan for *October Light*:

> I myself in a recent novel, *October Light*, began with the opin-
> ion that traditional New England values are the values we
> should live by ... and one tests those opinions in lifelike sit-
> uations, puts them under every kind of pressure one can
> think of, always being fair to the other side, and what one
> slowly discovers, resisting all the way, is that one's original
> opinion was oversimple [*Moral* 114].

Once again, the dialectic is at work in one of Gardner's novels. The thesis and antithesis of this particular dialectic can be seen as life lived in
the Page household versus life as portrayed in *Smugglers*. It can also be
seen as a dialectic between moral fiction — here represented by the main
novel sections of *October Light* versus *The Smugglers of Lost Souls' Rock*.
"*Smugglers'* main purpose in *October Light* is to contrast with the more
serious ... fiction that encompasses it," Dean McWilliams writes
(*Gardner* 85). Robert Morace agrees, writing, "The purpose of *The
Smugglers* section of *October Light* is to point out, in comic fashion, the
serious and harmful consequences for individuals and for society of
fiction that is not morally responsible. Clearly, it is not meant as an attack
on popular culture" ("New" 144).

For instance, one of the thorniest issues between James and Sally is
women's rights and the Equal Rights Amendment. Sally fancies herself
a feminist, while such beliefs are heresy for James. For her beliefs, Sally
is confined to the attic, where she reads about feminism run amok in
the character of Jane in *Smugglers*. Cowart pushes the relationship
between Sally and Jane even further: "Jane also seems to be a younger
version of Sally herself. Sally envies her sexual freedom and sees her own
situation mirrored in Jane's reluctant association with the captain"
(Cowart 114). The relationship between Jane and Sally forms the first
dialectic in the novel. Despite the *Deus-ex-machina* ending to *Smugglers*,
it becomes clear to Sally that there is a limit to how much one may promote feminism and remain (in Gardner's definition) moral.

David Cowart writes, "As Sally begins to realize that characters in
Smugglers resemble people in her own circle, the reader begins to apply
the heavy-handed symbolism of the novel-within-a-novel to the more
subtle thematic drift of the frame story" (*Arches* 112). Sally realizes that
she will be able to come to terms with James, but not as she was when
she was originally chased up into the attic. With her changed (but still

feminist) views, Sally is now ready to face James in what forms the second and more important dialectic in the novel. For James and Sally to come to any sort of agreement, however, James also will need to change. His own changes are brought about by the injuring of his daughter at Sally's hand, his own injuries sustained while driving drunk, and his guilt in bringing his friend Ed Thomas to a heart attack by holding a gun on him. James realizes that his actions have been rash — not just recently with Sally but throughout his whole life — and the old woman is finally able to emerge from the room upstairs with a new understanding of her brother.

As a brief coda, Gardner's penultimate novel, *Freddy's Book*, offers an image that can be construed as Arthurian, particularly when read with a knowledge of English literature in mind. *Freddy's Book* is oddly framed, with the novel being formed essentially from a short story — "Freddy" — and a novella, *King Gustav & the Devil*. The short story tells how Professor Winesap meets Professor Agaard and his son Freddy, who suffers from a glandular disorder that has rendered him a literal giant. The novella is one that Freddy has written and chronicles the rise to power, with the help of Satan, of King Gustav of Sweden. Principal among the characters is Gustav's knight Lars-Goren Bergquist, who fears the Devil and who knows, along with Bishop Brask (who represents the Catholic Church under assault by the Reformation), that the Devil must ultimately be eliminated and that this task will fall to Lars-Goren.

Very early in *King Gustav & the Devil*, Gardner establishes an important symbol in Bernt Notke's wooden statue of St. George killing the dragon. Later King Gustav will decide that, to stoke Swedish morale, the statue should tour the major cities of his kingdom. Freddy, as the narrator, writes that the statue represents "respectively, Sweden and her foreign enemies" (*Freddy's* 72). However, the event of St. George killing the dragon has stronger ties, for readers in English, to Spenser's *The Fairie Queene*, the first book of which culminates in the Red Cross Knight — at that late juncture revealed as St. George — slaying the dragon, which symbolizes any number of sixteenth-century England's political foes: the Catholic Church, France, Spain. And because of the repeated appearances in *The Faerie Queene* of Prince Arthur, here in the image of St. George killing the dragon we have a symbol with some Arthurian resonance. At the very least, St. George is far more readily identifiable as patron saint of England than of Sweden.

When Lars-Goren returns to his home briefly to visit with his family, he decides to take them to Hudiksvall, where the statue is at that time being displayed. Gardner's description of the statue indicates his knowledge that the image of St. George killing the dragon is one that goes beyond simple Swedish symbolism:

> What he saw was the blank, staring face of the knight, gazing straight forward, motionless, as if indifferent to the monster, gazing as if mad or entranced or blind, infinitely gentle, infinitely sorrowful, beyond all human pain. I am Sweden, he seemed to say — or something more than Sweden. *I am humanity, living and dead.* For it did not seem to Lars-Goren that the monster below the belly of the violently trembling horse could be described as, simply, "foreigners," as the common interpretation maintained. It was evil itself; death, oblivion, every conceivable form of human loss [*Freddy's* 147, emphasis original].

McWilliams writes, "Lars-Goren reads the statue morally, and it provides a commentary on the task he will soon set for himself. Saint George kills evil" (*Gardner* 95).

Lars-Goren's son Erik is particularly taken with the statue and the journey to see it. Along the way, he sees the remnants of burned witches and declares that when he is a knight, he will not allow witches to be burned. However, this is an activity that Lars-Goren has been involved in during his own tenure as a knight. Thus there is a sharp contrast between the father's and the son's concepts of knightly chivalry. Cowart sums up the relationship in an explicitly Arthurian fashion: In introducing Erik and his aspirations, Gardner hints at the emergence of a line of heroes, a self-sustaining heroic ideal. But he also hints at a moral distinction between father and son, who thus resemble another pair of related heroes. Lancelot, morally compromised by the affair with Guinevere, falls short of the ideal attained by his son, the stainless Galahad, and Lars-Goren and Erik seem to follow the same pattern (Cowart 158).

The final lines of *Freddy's Book* offer one last indication that Gardner intended a broader meaning for his novel than simply the story of a Swedish king's rise to power and a knight's private battle against evil. "Now the red of the sky was fading," Gardner writes. "In Russia, the tsar, with ice on his eyelashes, was declaring war on Poland. 'Little do they dream,' he said, 'what horrors they've unleashed on themselves, daring to think lightly of the tsar!' All around him, his courtiers bowed humbly, their palms and fingertips touching as if for prayer" (*Freddy's* 245). Lars-Goren has managed to kill the Devil by this last page of the novel, but a threat still exists from the East. It is through this threat that Gardner is perhaps alluding to his own times, when the Soviet Union maintained a tense relationship with the U.S. In fact, *Freddy's Book* appeared when the Soviet-aligned communist government of Poland was suffering the turmoil of dealing with the Solidarity labor movement, so tension between Russia and Poland was a relevant topic for Gardner to choose here. Just as St. George kills the dragon but the threat of evil always exists, Lars-Goren kills the very personification of evil, but evil remains elsewhere in the world.

Gardner followed up *Freddy's Book* with *Mickelsson's Ghosts*, which like *The Resurrection* used as its source material philosophical texts — in this case, mainly Nietzsche. In 1982, while at work on two novels, *Stillness* and *Shadows*, Gardner was killed in a motorcycle accident. (The works have since been released in their unfinished forms.) He left behind a legacy of work that sought to instruct the reader in moral behavior and living — a vast departure from his contemporaries. Gardner's contribution to American Arthuriana is essentially that offered by Steinbeck: a model at once to be held as an ideal and to be debased because of its incongruity with modern times. Gardner, however, was more subtle in his usage of the source texts in question, never offering a purely Arthurian work on the lines of *Tortilla Flat*. As we shall see, one of Gardner's contemporaries, Donald Barthelme, also chose to use Arthurian myths and legends as a kind of sounding board for the excesses of modern times, but he decided to aim for humor and irony rather than morality. Gardner was never able to make his vision of moral fiction the prevailing form, even when he relied on one of English literature's most enduring legends to do so.

CHAPTER VII

Donald Barthelme, et al.

Donald Barthelme's *The King* is among the most recent Arthurian works by a major American writer, and the novel offers a unique counterpoint to Twain's *A Connecticut Yankee in King Arthur's Court*. In Barthelme's work, anachronism is put to use as thoroughly as in Twain's novel, but the implementation of the device is reversed: Instead of a modern man sent into the sixth century to meet Arthur and the Knights of the Round Table, Arthur, Launcelot, Guinevere, and the others appear in modern Europe during World War II. This difference notwithstanding, Barthelme's engagement of cultural, social, and political issues in his inverted text is no less extensive than Twain's. For instance, *The King* is as much a comment on society — particularly literary society — at the end of the twentieth century as *Connecticut Yankee* was on the nineteenth. Furthermore, although *The King* was published after Barthelme's death from cancer in 1989, he was writing the novel while the world was on the cusp between the Cold War and the new world order in which the U.S. became the world's sole superpower. The novel takes place at a similar border — between World War II and the Cold War — and thus the political situations the novel addresses reverberate throughout the latter half of the century. Reading *The King* in the context of these historical events, along with a few other similarly Arthurian texts, will render these relationships more clear.

Barthelme was a postmodernist, and insofar as one of postmodernism's goals is the debasement of modernism, Barthelme's postmodernist sensibilities are alive and well in *The King*. Part of the author's project, therefore, is to show how and why modernism failed as a movement, and in doing so, he links these reasons to the social and political climate during World War II — all within an Arthurian framework. Thus the most prominent symbol of modernism's failure in *The King* becomes the war itself. World War II served as the *coup de grace* for modernism as it laid waste not only to Europe but to its artistic traditions as well. This was clear, among other ways, in the deaths of James Joyce and Virginia Woolf in the early years of the war, the disintegration of Ezra Pound into war propagandist, and Pound's eventual commitment to a mental institution. As a result, Barthelme and the postmodernists must make do with the legacy of an exhausted tradition, and John Domini writes that Barthelme attributes the failure of the movement to the war by "going back to where the breakup began" (Domini 108), as happens in *The King.* Thus we see that Barthelme traces the deficiency of literary forms since World War II to the decline of modernism.

For instance, in depicting Pound's real-life wartime broadcasts, replete with anti-Semitic epithets, Barthelme vividly shows the debasement of the modernist author. A typical passage serves as an example:

> The Bolshevik anti-morale," said Ezra, "comes out of the Talmud, which is the dirtiest teaching that any race ever codified. The Talmud is the one and only begetter of the Bolshevik system."
>
> "In a moment he'll be talking about 'kikified usurers,'" said Arthur. "One expects poets to be mad, but —"
>
> "He reminds me," said Sir Kay, "of some old country squire, in Surrey somewhere, running on after dinner to his poor bedraggled wife."
>
> "I suppose one could knit to this," Arthur said. "It would induce concentration."
>
> "You would do better to innoculate your children with typhus and syphilis," said Ezra, "than to let in the Sassoons, Rothschilds, and Warburgs" [*King* 7].

Significantly, Pound is discounting a text in this tirade. Equally important is that Pound's assessment of the Talmud is completely incorrect. The Talmud actually devotes several tractates to the disposition of private property and its protection. Ironically, if there is any religious text that engenders collectivism the most, it is probably the New Testament. At this point, Pound was no longer writing poetry but propagandizing over the radio. (He would return to poetry and produce his very fine *Pisan Cantos* while awaiting trial for treason.) Through this action, we see that when the poet stops producing texts, the result is chaos. Also we see the deterioration of the modernist author publicly as Arthur expresses a common perception of the poet as insane. The king's assessment itself is a debasement of the classical notion of the poet as divinely inspired.

It is historical accuracy that dictates Pound's presence in the novel, but that Pound was a writer so consistently obsessed with myth is particularly convenient for Barthelme's project. In a previous novel, *The Dead Father*, Barthelme had symbolized the decline of myth in the burial of the Dead Father, with all its Freudian implications, at the end of the novel. Similarly, the exhaustion of myth is an integral element of *The King*. Larry McCaffery has suggested that the most problematic aspect of using myth in postmodern fiction is "a self-consciousness about myth that has reached such paralyzing proportions that most contemporary use of myth is overtly self-conscious and is employed primarily for comic purposes" (McCaffery 21). *The King* faces this difficulty because it is a novel-length allusion to Arthurian myth. In a way, though, the novel serves as the end of the line for this exhausted allusion since, as Thomas M. Leitch points out, "[T]he better an audience already knows a narrative, the less concerned it is that the narrator get to the point" ("Barthelme" 142). By using a literary source that is among the oldest possible in the English-language tradition, Barthelme would be unlikely to reach the point to which Leitch refers. The result, in theory, would be a text without point or purpose and therefore very unstable. The postmodern novel is thereby successful.

While it is questionable whether or not the case of *The King* is as extreme as this, the use of such an ancient allusion as the primary focus of a postmodern text is still highly problematic. McCaffery posits, writing on *Snow White*, that Barthelme uses allusions parodically to show the exhaustion of language (McCaffery 31). Again, we see an idea taken to extreme in *The King*, as Barthelme places characters using medieval vernacular during the 1930s and 1940s:

> "I have slain upwards of thirty authentic dragons, but I told the *Times* fellow not to put that in the paper."
>
> "Furthermore," said Walter the Penniless, "have you noticed what the king's been up to lately? Been acting a little strange, Arthur, hasn't he? Have you chaps been paying attention? Or is he just too noble and grand to answer for his actions like other kings?"
>
> "Shall we brast his pate or give him a few pennies?" asked Sir Roger.
>
> "The latter, I think. Deprive him of his rationale. I've got two pounds six."
>
> "I've got three pounds."
>
> The knights showering money on Walter the Penniless [40].

Here Barthelme milks the juxtaposition of medieval language and symbols to a modern setting for all its comic possibilities. Launcelot brags of killing dragons to a modern *Times* reporter, and then the knights deliberate over "brasting Water's pate" or giving him modern currency. Anachronism is Barthelme's chief comic device here, and though King George VI has been supplanted by Arthur, Winston Churchill is still the prime minister, though he ironically suggests, as Norris Lacy points out, that Arthur "is not a man for the current season" (Lacy 164).

Barthelme's assault on Pound shows the bankruptcy of modernism through his discrediting of that movement's foremost figures. But beyond Pound, Barthelme also uses myth as a link to modernism and a similar critique of that literary tradition, in this way cutting the modernist movement down to size and disempowering modernist texts (Domini 99). In *The Dead Father,* Barthelme used repeated allusions to James Joyce's *Finnegan's Wake* to establish a link between myth and modernism (Domini 102). In *The King,* Barthleme develops this link more fully and attacks it more vigorously. In one sense, the debasement of the Grail legend is itself a poke at modernism, particularly at Eliot and *The Waste Land.* As we shall see, the Hanged Man who appears in *The Waste Land* makes an appearance in Barthelme's novel. His inclusion of this figure from the Tarot in his work is no less arbitrary than Eliot's association of the Tarot with Grail figures, as the latter admits in his notes to *The Waste Land.* "The Man with Three Staves (an authentic member of the Tarot pack) I associate, quite arbitrarily, with the Fisher King himself," Eliot writes in a footnote (*Waste* 5ff).

In his essay "Not-Knowing," Barthelme poses a series of rhetorical questions: "What is the complicity of language in the massive crimes of fascism...? If these abominations are all in some sense facilitated by ... language, to what degree is that language ruinously contaminated?" (*Voicelust* 42). In *The King,* he answers by affirming language's complicity, or ambiguity at best. The author shows this by frequently juxtaposing Pound's invectives with those of Lord Haw-Haw — the pseudonym of the British traitor William Joyce, who spent the war in the Third Reich broadcasting pro-Axis material to English-speaking radio listeners. The irony is that while Pound's speeches are mostly lies, Lord Haw-Haw speaks the truth more often than not: At this point in the war, the Nazis really are winning, and Guinevere really is sleeping with Launcelot. In this way, Barthelme shows not only the corruption of the language of the literary artist but the disappearance of truth from the voice of the poet.

Barthelme continues in *The King* the development of other ideas introduced in *The Dead Father* and *Snow White*. For instance, the age-old theme of the son's deposition of the father, seen in *The Dead Father* in Thomas's burial of the literally statuesque Dead Father and in *The King* (not to mention in all of Arthurian literature) in Mordred's betrayal of Arthur and in his alignment with the Nazis.

More important, however, is the theme of anachronism in these novels. In *The Dead Father*, Barthelme deals with, among other themes, the outdated value of religion and belief in God (the Dead Father) in contemporary culture. In *Snow White*, the author shows the obsolescence of fairy tales in times that are far from innocent. In *The King*, there is the sociopolitical anachronism of the monarchy in modern times.

By replacing the actual monarchy of George VI with King Arthur and the Knights of the Round Table, Barthelme gives the anachronism a literary twist. Through the connection drawn between Arthurian legend and the anachronism central to the novel, Barthelme makes a strong statement concerning the anachronism of texts in a contemporary culture that offers such non-literary media as radio and television. Barthelme himself was aware of the decline of the writer in contemporary culture. In a 1982 interview, he lamented the ubiquity of the telephone because, as he stated, "[W]e don't even write letters anymore. I don't write letters—I don't even write business letters. I call up on the telephone. When people don't write letters, language deteriorates" (Brans 125). Barthelme could perceive the effects of the decline of the writer and he realized that when writing loses importance in a society, the quality of that society's literature suffers.

Such gloomy forecasts notwithstanding, Barthelme relies on several traditional motifs of the Arthurian tales in conveying the political and historical themes of *The King*, notably the designations of knights by color. There is a Black Knight, a Blue Knight, a Red Knight, a Yellow Knight, and a Brown Knight, as well as Launcelot, Kay, Bedivere, and others. One of the least typical Arthurian constructions in *The King* is the way Barthelme represents the Holy Grail. In a characteristic scene, the Black Knight (Sir Roger de Ibadan) and the Blue Knight discuss the significance of the Grail to the war effort. The Blue Knight deduces that the modern Grail must be a bomb, saying, "A bomb, I think ... A really horrible bomb. One more horrible and powerful and despicable than any bomb ever made before. Capable of unparalleled destruction and the most hideous effect on human life." The Black Knight replies that it "seems far removed from the Grail of old" (*King* 77). Thus the salvation that this bomb will bring, if it can be found, will be victory over the Nazis, although as in the original history the Germans are searching for it also.

The depiction of the Grail as an object of destructive potential is a grave variation on the medieval versions of the story, but this characterization does not begin with Barthelme. Indeed, the association is seen in several postwar pulp-fiction novels, for instance. But it is likely that the text exerting more influence on Barthelme was Thomas Pynchon's *Gravity's Rainbow.*

The basic Grail element in this 1973 novel is Tyrone Slothrop's quest in the final days of World War II to find Rocket 00000, one of the V-2 rockets that Nazi Germany had been firing at England since 1943. (As the third part of the novel takes place in the days immediately before Hiroshima and the fourth part immediately following, there is also some connection to the atom bomb.) Slothrop has a personal stake in his quest in that every place a V-2 has landed in London has been, before the fact, the site of a sexual encounter of his.

The specific Arthurian references that Pynchon makes in connection with the bomb/Grail quest are relatively few and are widely dispersed throughout the text. The earliest comes in a reference to Eliot's *The Waste Land,* which, thanks to Steinbeck and other earlier writers, has become a principal intertext for American writers of Arthuriana. During a séance attended by Roger Mexico and Jessica Swanlake, Jessica recalls that in 1936 Pirate Prentice, who is also attending the séance, had been in love with a woman named Scorpia Mossmoon. She dubs the period a "T.S. Eliot April" (Pynchon 35), referring to the first line of *The Waste Land,* though it was, in fact, earlier in the winter.

Bruce Sublett has written that the relationship between *The Waste Land* and *Gravity's Rainbow* is cultural: "*The Waste Land* brought myth to bear on the Lost Generation; *Gravity's Rainbow* recasts the same myth for the Love Generation [hippies]" (Sublett 9). Thus placing this reference to Eliot's poem in the context of the séance links another baby-boomer fad (séances) with larger mythic constructs, or what Sublett calls "expand[ing] the mythological themes modeled by Eliot, themes of universal import" (Sublett 94).

Sublett elaborates on this relationship by pointing out the references to President John F. Kennedy in the text (Sublett 43). Slothrop had been in Kennedy's class at Harvard, and this association is one way of providing an even greater connection to children of the 1960s, who remembered JFK fondly and saw America's loss of innocence in his assassination. Elsewhere Pynchon connects Slothrop to Malcolm X (also assassinated), and Sublett suggests that offering both mainstream and counterculture counterparts for his protagonist allows Pynchon to expound more broadly on Slothrop's "potential as a '60s myth figure ... enhanced by his connection with two bona-fide '60s folk-heros [*sic*]" (Sublett 67). In the case of Kennedy, this association is enhanced by the posthumous dubbing of his presidency as Camelot.

The juxtaposition of the séance with the allusion from Eliot is also important because it speaks to one of the broader devices Pynchon uses in the novel — the Tarot — which is also used extensively by Eliot. Steven Weisenburger writes that the entire first section of the novel is informed by the Tarot; for instance, there are twenty-one sub-sections in this section and the Tarot deck has twenty-one cards if one removes the Fool (i.e., Slothrop) from the deck (Weisenburger 15). More important and more specifically Arthurian would be the Tarot symbolically thrown for Slothrop near the end of the novel. Also, the parts of the novel that take place in the Zone, i.e., the Allied Zone of occupation in immediate post-war Germany, are linked by setting to Eliot. Sublett notes that both Eliot's Waste Land and the Zone are "man-made hell[s] that may be beyond redemption" (Sublett 75) and that the Zone serves the same purpose as a symbol of the "sterility of human emotion" for baby-boomers that Eliot's setting served for the Lost Generation (76).

Eliot receives another nod from Pynchon through the character of Blicero, who along with his homosexual lover, Gottfried, will launch Rocket 00000 at the novel's end. An auxiliary character, Thanatz, encounters Blichero and notes that he is "out by the shelled and rusty gasworks" (Pynchon 776). Sublett notes that this line echoes one from *The Waste Land* that refers to the Fisher King, who is "fishing in the dull canal ... round behind the gashouse" (Sublett 189-90). Sublett further notes that Blicero propagates a form of sterility in his non-reproductive couplings with Gottfried (Sublett 38). This sterility is inherent to the Grail story and extends, in Pynchon's novel, to other characters, notably Marvy, who is castrated when he is mistaken for Slothrop and taken captive. The other persons thus characterized are the *Schwarzkommando*, the black African partisans fighting for the Axis and searching for their own rocket during the Allied occupation, who after two generations under the yoke of German colonialism have given up on procreative forms of sex. That the *Schwarzkommando* are symbolic Grail questers adds another level of significance to their sterility (Sublett 37).

During a digression on the origins of the *Schwarzkommando,* Pynchon drops another Arthurian reference. Much of the section concerns the self-destructive impulse among the *Schwarzkommando* and how this impulse relates to the science of rocketry — symbolized for both by the concept of the Final Zero. Two *Schwarzkommando* leaders, Enzian and Ombindi, are discussing this relationship, and the narrator comments:

> Still [Ombindi] will profess it and proclaim it, as an image of a grail slipping through the room, radiant, though the jokers around the table will be sneaking Whoopee Cushions into the Siege Perilous, under the very descending arse of the grailseeker, and though the grails themselves come in plastic these years, a dime a dozen, penny a gross, still Ombindi, at times self-conned as any Christian, praises and prophesies that era of innocence he just missed living in ... [Pynchon 321].

The Grail myth is doubly profaned here, in its relationship to self-destructive paraphilias and in the reduction of the Siege Perilous — the seat of the Round Table reserved for the knight who will attain the Grail — to a fart joke.

Significantly, Pynchon, in making reference to the "image of a grail slipping through a room" is alluding specifically to Launcelot's experience as a Grail knight, being able to see the Grail but not actually win it. Thus the *Schwarzkommando* are in the position of being unsuitable Grail knights, though for different reasons than Launcelot. Slothrop's own unsuitability as a Grail knight is attested to in numerous ways, most notably in his broad sexuality in comparison to the traditional chastity of Grail knights like Percival and Galahad. Elsewhere, as when Slothrop undertakes the quest-within-the-quest of retrieving hashish from Potsdam, the ideal of the Grail quest is further profaned (Sublett 3). Slothrop seems to sense his own unsuitability, as when he thinks, "The Schwarzgerät [literally black device — the black apparatus that may explain Slothrop's sexual connection to the rockets] is no Grail, Ace, that's not what that G in Imipolex G [a erectile plastic used in constructing the rocket that may also explain Slothrop's connection] stands for" (Pynchon 364). That the Grail is associated with weapons of destruction is a further debasement of the myth of the Grail as restorative relic.

However, another compound, methyl methacrylate, is dubbed "a replica of the Sangraal" (Pynchon 487).

If Slothrop resembles Launcelot in his ability to see the Grail but not attain it, Sublett posits an even stronger relationship between Slothrop and Percival, particularly as characterized in Wolfram von Eschenbach's *Parsifal*. For example, just as Parsifal comes from an aristocratic (i.e., knightly) family but loses his social status when he loses his father, Slothrop (like Pynchon) comes from a Mayflower family whose fortunes have fallen on hard times thanks to poor business decisions (Sublett 42-43). Similarly, Parsifal's quest is marked by successive encounters with women that seem increasingly pointless. In Slothrop this pattern becomes explicitly sexual (unlike the chaste Parsifal) but no less pointless (Sublett 46-47).

Sublett writes that Parsifal is "portrayed ludicrously in the beginning, and his counterpart Gawain remains a relatively comic figure throughout the work. Wolfram's intent was probably to maintain audience interest, and he did so by interspersing comedy with high drama" (Sublett 33). Thus comedy in Pynchon's Grail quest is appropriate if we consider Wolfram as his precedent. Sublett notes further that, just as in Wolfram, Parsifal becomes less inspired in his quest, so does Slothrop become more and more bored in trying to find Rocket 00000: "His Grail draws him on inexorably, yet the nearer he comes to it, the less actively he pursues it" (Sublett 36).

The Grail associations do not end here; there are many Grails and many Grail questers in *Gravity's Rainbow* and most are a far cry from their mythic prototypes. This is established in the line that points out that "grails themselves come in plastic these days, a dime a dozen, a penny a gross ..." (Pynchon 373). For instance, Dr. Pointsman, the Pavlovian psychologist involved in Slothrop's case, has the Nobel Prize as his Grail. Enzian's half-brother Tchitcherine, the Soviet intelligence agent, is on a Grail quest of sorts also — specifically to find Enzian and kill him, though on the surface his quest is the same as Slothrop's: to gather information on the rocket. The violent nature of this quest alone is enough to further degrade the myth, but like Steinbeck's many Grail knights, Tchitcherine does not reach his goal. He is put under a spell by Katje and he passes by Enzian without even recognizing him — one of several anticlimaxes in the novel. This anticlimax is paired with Slothrop's own inability to find Rocket 00000.

In the final section of *Gravity's Rainbow*, we get Slothrop's symbolic Tarot, thrown metaphorically to conclude his fate in the novel. The narrator notes, "All his hopeful cards are reversed, most unhappily of all the Hanged Man, who is supposed to be upside down to begin with, telling of his secret hopes and fears ..." (Pynchon 738). Weisenburger, using the Paine method of reading Tarot that Pynchon specifically pre-scribes, concludes that the throw signifies "the satiric treatment Pynchon has given Slothrop's role as mock-Orpheus" (Weisenburger 306). This image is juxtaposed with one on the following page, once again linking the Rocket to the Holy Grail: "The Grail, the Sangraal, is the bloody vehicle" (Pynchon 739). It is a fitting metaphor, since the Rocket causes bloodshed and the Grail was the vessel that held Jesus's blood. The prox-imity of these images also calls to mind *The Waste Land,* both generally, because it is a Grail-themed work, and specifically, because that poem also contains the image of the Hanged Man. And, as we shall see, the metaphor links Pynchon's novel to Barthelme's.

There are other areas of thematic overlap between *Gravity's Rainbow* and *The King.* For instance, beyond the simple Grail-as-bomb metaphor that both novels share, there is also the frantic racing by multiple par-ties toward a shared goal. As such, the race for the Grail, whether it is Barthelme's atom bomb or Pynchon's V-2, prefigures the arms race that would characterize the Cold War, from Los Alamos and the Soviet acqui-sition of the atomic bomb in 1949, through the hydrogen bomb con-troversy, the Cuban Missile Crisis, the SALT talks, and U.S.-Soviet détente. The whole process was building up to critical mass under the Reagan Administration, and these developments were the most signi-ficant for Barthelme while he was writing *The King,* particularly the need to consider such weapons with the shifting of power in post-Cold War Europe. Pynchon's text contains a Russian (Tchitcherine) questing for the Grail, and the competition between him and the other knights in *Gravity's Rainbow* creates a similar sort of tension.

Furthermore, both Pynchon and Barthelme debase the Grail myth by turning the religious relic, traditionally a symbol of rebirth and revi-talization, into a weapon of mass destruction and a harbinger of geno-cide. There is no less urgency in the chase for the Grail among the characters of *Gravity's Rainbow,* since their search for the rocket is impor-tant to the future control of the Allied Zone of Occupation in postwar Germany and, extending outwards, all of Europe. There are also broader cultural and historical references to be found in *Gravity's Rainbow;* for example, the aforementioned link between Slothrop and JFK. Kennedy is an apt symbol of nuclear brinkmanship, considering his handling of the Cuban Missile Crisis.

Returning to *The King*, the Grail-as-bomb metaphor is carried forward when Sir Percy Plangent writes an opera entitled *The Grail*. Its plot is summarized thus: "In Act One, it [the Grail/bomb] is discovered. In Act Two, it is refined. In Act Three, it explodes!" (*King* 101). But here a different explanation is given for the long-term implications of the development of the Grail/bomb. We are told, "The bomb is a metaphor for the unhappiness of those groaning under the yoke" (King 101). Just exactly what this yoke is can be read in several different ways. First, there are the obvious sufferings of the peasantry under an autocrat such as Hitler or Stalin, or the general populace under the great war. This particular type of oppression, and the response to it, is symbolized in several characters. First, there is the Red Knight, Sir Ironside of the Red Lands, who speaks admiringly of "[t]he Party [that] embodies the collective wisdom of the people [and that] has access to information the individual doesn't have" (*King* 62). Clearly the Red Knight symbolizes European communism and in particular its subordination of personal need to the requirements of the Party. That he is more specifically a symbol of Soviet communism is revealed in his remarks about the "Teutonic hordes" that will soon cross his borders, as well as in the Black Knight's needling of the Red Knight about the "'37 trials"—the Stalinist purges in the years preceding World War II.

Beyond the communist example, we must also consider, in regard to the *Grail* play, the suffering of the general populace under the yoke of a military-industrial complex the likes of which would be created in part by the development of the bomb and similar weapons. Furthermore, we are told that Sir Roger — the Black Knight — feels particularly torn by the play, and it is through this unique character that we can understand another postwar geopolitical implication that Barthelme is introducing here. One clue to this special relationship between the Black Knight and Camelot comes while the court is listening to one of the broadcasts from Lord Haw-Haw. In one episode, Joyce (Haw-Haw) speaks about race in England and concludes, "There are too many Negroes in Britain .... Your in-migration from Egypt, India, the Caribbean, and God knows where is ruining the country." What Joyce leaves out of his diatribe is that — for better or for worse — there are so many non-whites in Britain because of British colonialism, which we may consider as another "yoke" under which the people may be "groaning."

Not coincidentally, Launcelot brings up the Black Knight in the very same scene in which Joyce is broadcasting about race. Launcelot asks Arthur if he's ever met a "truly black knight" (*King* 108). When Arthur answers that he hasn't, Launcelot tells him about Roger. Earlier in the novel, when Launcelot first meets Roger, Launcelot learns that he comes from Dahomey in West Africa, though the Black Knight will variously refer to his homeland as either Dahomey or by its post-colonial name, Benin. What is important to note here is that the Black Knight personifies the dissolution of the British Empire with the rise of African — and to a lesser extent South Asian — nationalism. Like the eventual ruling classes in the nations that received independence between 1948 and 1961, the Black Knight is well-educated, English-speaking, and has managed to enter the social strata of the British aristocracy. As such, he would be a prime candidate for a role in the government of any post-colonial national entity. And the inherent problem in this relationship would be that, as history has shown, what ultimately results from the passing of power from the colonialists to those who worked most closely with the colonialists is merely more corruption. One likely reaction to such corruption would be Marxism, and the Black Knight does note that Africa "has a fair number of Reds" (*King* 38), perhaps a nod to the future collectivization in Angola.

It should also be noted that the use of a bona fide black man to fill the role of the mythical Black Knight is not Barthelme's innovation. The practice is actually fairly common in American literature, where black characters have traditionally played a more significant part along with their white counterparts. In the post-World War II era, the conceit has been used not only by Pynchon, whose *Schwarzkommando* can be seen as an entire legion of "black knights," but also by Walker Percy, perhaps most famous for writing *The Moviegoer.* In his 1977 novel *Lancelot*, Percy reconstructs the Grail quest — here a quest for the knowledge of the true paternity of the protagonist's child — in a particularly lurid mode, as told by the protagonist to his confessor-priest, conveniently nicknamed Percival. Similarly, the title character, though ostensibly named for Lancelot Andrewes, the chief translator of the King James Bible, is an obvious stand-in for his Arthurian namesake, as is one of the auxiliary characters, Robert Merlin. There is much in the character of Lance (as he is generally called in the novel) to suggest a knightly character. For instance, he is descended from Confederate generals, and in his own time he was a hero on the football field. But at the same time, as an attorney during the 1960s, he stood against popular opinion and helped integrate his native New Orleans, so this nobility is not just genetic or physical but character-based as well.

However, by the time of the action of the novel, Lance has fallen from grace. Part of this fall is his discovery that it is literally impossible, based on the results of blood tests, for him to be the father of his daughter by his second wife, Margot. He becomes obsessed with finding out with whom his wife is really sleeping, but he realizes that he is not personally fit for such a quest. Therefore, he enlists the help of Elgin, the child of his black servants, in fulfilling his quest. The contrast between Lance and his "black knight" is more than just a question of color. While Lance dictates the action that Elgin will undertake, he recognizes, as Lewis Lawson writes, that he is "a dirty and disgraced Sir Lancelot" (Lawson 756). Nonetheless, like any knight preparing to undertake a quest, Lance bathes and undergoes tests of his stamina. Elgin, however, is already clean-cut and thus ready for the quest. Elgin tells his employer he'd do "anything you axed" (Percy 81), and this African-American locution reveals another flaw in Lance's character — as much as he has done to help Southern blacks, he still holds them as inherently inferior, and his personal reaction to Elgin's pronunciation reveals this attitude.

Lance and Elgin plan to hide cameras in the bedrooms of his house, where Margot, who is an actress, is working on a film with the aforementioned director, Robert Merlin. The planning and execution of the secret filming bring out further details of the quest at hand. For instance, Elgin is "armed" with a secret, "magical" weapon: Realizing the difficulty of the task, he suggests to Lance that he use a "Kiefer blacklight stylus," to which Lance replies, "You do that" (Percy 92). Lance gives Elgin a layout of the bedrooms he is to film, and the servant immediately dubs the layout a "map." Lawson makes much of this terminology, citing poet W.H. Auden's own discussion of the Grail-questing elements behind much detective fiction. Lawson thus quotes Auden, "In the detective story, as in its mirror image, the Quest for the Grail, maps (the ritual of space) and timetables (the ritual of time) are desirable" (Lawson 756).

At the novel's end, all the infidelities are revealed, and in a revenge-driven, murderous rage, Lance destroys his own house by causing a gas leak and then blowing it up, thus killing most of the people inside and confining himself to the institution from which he makes his "confession." Elgin's role in the tragedy ends with the surveillance, however, and so he is not nearly so complicitous in the sad ending as is his employer. Thus this "black knight" proves himself loyal to his employer/king and helps bring the action of the novel to its tragic conclusion. In Malory, Launcelot was a Grail knight, but it was left to Galahad to finally recover the Grail. Similarly, in *Lancelot*, Lance cannot complete the task at hand; only Elgin, representing Galahad, is successful.

More recently, John Updike has used the symbol of the African Black Knight in his novel *Brazil*, an updating of the Tristan and Isolde romance. The subject of Tristan and Isolde is one that Updike first covered in a mid-1960s short story, "Four Sides of One Story," in which Tristran, Iseult of the White Hands, Iseult the Fair, and King Mark each write about their views on their unfortunate scenario. Much of the humor in this short piece is similar to Barthelme's in *The King* (and Twain's in *Connecticut Yankee*)— the use of anachronism and the juxtaposition of the medieval and the modern. For instance, the potion that binds Tristan to Iseult is transformed into a Daiquiri consumed in a bar. Furthermore, in a letter Iseult of the White Hands laments, "This way of life we've all been living doesn't conduce to much spare time. I haven't read a book or magazine in weeks. Now the brats are asleep (I think), the dishes are chugging away in the washer, and here I sit with my fifth glass of Noilly Prat for the day" ("Four Sides" 94). Iseult the Fair complains that she has "lost 12 pounds and live[s] on pills— I dismay myself" ("Four Sides" 97).

Updike dispenses with such incongruities in *Brazil*. In this version of the Tristan legend, Tristan is Tristao, a black Brazilian, and Isolde is Isabel, his white lover. (We should probably note here that Ysobel is the name given by Steinbeck to his femme fatale in *Cup of Gold*, so perhaps Updike's naming convention is a nod to the earlier writer.) Unlike in Percy's novel or even in *The King*, where race is not the principal theme, in *Brazil* nearly all the action is inspired by Tristao and Isabel's need to flee her family because of their displeasure at Tristao's being a black man. While Updike characterizes Tristao— at least initially — as a hoodlum who mugs tourists, he is nonetheless frequently called "chivalrous" in the narration, and the author endows Tristao's weapon of choice, a razor he calls "Gem," with a certain magical medieval sensibility. Furthermore, the language Tristao and Isabel use with each other is stilted and arcane, despite the frequently mundane topics of conversation, for example, Tristao's observation that because "[t]he poor grow such thick skins, the loving touch has to be heavy" (*Brazil* 244). While there is no potion in *Brazil* to speak of, magic does play an important part in the plot. In the Brazilian bush, the lovers fall afoul of a lost group of Portuguese colonists unaware after many generations that slavery has been abolished. Tristao is enslaved and put to work making canoes, while Isabel is forced to marry one of the colonists. To free Tristao, she agrees to undergo a process by an Indian shaman that eventually changes both hers and Tristao's races, with the end result being that Isabel is black and Tristao is white. Tristao is no longer a "black knight," but he remains a knight to the end. Thus we can see that Barthelme is not the only author to use the conceit of the "black knight" in American literature, though he is the only writer who uses the concept to suggest not Western obsessions with race but rather incipient anti-colonialist and nationalist movements in Africa.

Back in Barthelme's Europe, Arthur and his knights are forced to deal with the rising nationalism sweeping not just Africa but Europe as well with the rise and early successes of the Axis powers. This was particularly the case in Eastern Europe, where the Nazis took a divide-and-conquer approach to the Slavic states. In the case of Czechoslovakia, for instance, Hitler annexed Bohemia and Moravia and created a newly independent and pro-Axis Slovakia. Like the nationalism of Africa, the nationalism inspired by the Axis would extend beyond the war years, despite attempts by postwar politicians to prevent it. An exchange between Guinevere and Varley, one of her servants, early in the novel is particularly significant:

> "One has to think about so many different sorts of people one never thought about before," Guinevere said. "Croats, for example. I never knew there was such a thing as a Croat before this war."
> "Are they on our side?"
> "As I understand it, they are being held in reserve for a possible uprising in the event that the Serbs fail to live up to some agreement or other."
> "What's a Serb, mum?" [*King* 5].

The Nazis' policy in Yugoslavia was quite similar to that in Czechoslovakia: Croatia became a puppet state, while Serbia fell under Italian and German occupation. In the years after World War II, Marshall Josef Tito, the communist dictator of Yugoslavia and a Croat, sought to ease ethnic tensions in his country by outlawing displays of nationalism.

However, as the world is all too aware in recent years, this policy did nothing but render these tensions temporarily impotent. With Tito's death in 1980 and the ten years between his death and the rise of Slobodan Milosevic, decaying ethnic relations in Yugoslavia were a harbinger of things to come. By focusing Guinevere and Varley's conversation on nationalities like the Serbs and Croats, Barthelme is perhaps acknowledging this perennial powder keg in Europe.

The development of the bomb project by the British serves as a good example of what a political hot potato atomic weaponry will become — within the confines of the novel and beyond. In one of the more bizarre scenes in *The King,* Sir Launcelot and the Black Knight are wandering through a forest and come upon a man suspended from a tree by his leg — the figure of the Hanged Man as presented in the Tarot (and in *The Waste Land* and *Gravity's Rainbow*). After Launcelot cuts the Hanged Man down and sets him free, the Black Knight notices that the Hanged Man has mathematical equations written on his leg and he copies them down. Now that the Hanged Man is free to wander, he is next seen at an oration by Walter the Penniless, another of the novel's characters symbolizing Marxist thought. The Hanged Man is depicted as being sympathetic to Walter's communist principles, as is the Yellow Knight (perhaps a crude symbol of the Asian attraction to Marxism, particularly in China), who comes across his own set of equations that are also used in developing the atomic weapon.

Much later in the novel, the Black Knight is at a meeting with Launcelot, Arthur, Sir Kay, and the Blue Knight, and he declares that the equations found both on the Hanged Man's leg and in the possession of the Yellow Knight "will enable us to build a bomb more powerful than any the world has ever known." He concludes, "It's the Grail you chaps have been seeking. The big boom" (*King* 76). There follows a debate on how the bomb should be used. Some suggest that it could be used against Mordred, who has risen up against his father and has aligned himself with the Axis; other knights suggest the bomb be used against Germany and Italy proper. Sir Kay's suggestion that it be deployed against a smaller city — Essen and Kiel are his suggestions — is reminiscent of similar debates among Allied generals on the subject of not using the bomb against Japan without appropriate warning — for instance, the bombing of a nearby atoll. Arthur decides that the Grail is not a "knightly weapon" and destroys the equations before him. Of course, the received history of the war dictates that the Americans will develop the bomb instead and will deploy it against Hiroshima and Nagasaki, but since the scope of the novel does not fall beyond 1941, this information is merely hinted at and not worked explicitly into the plot. However, we may consider that the American scientific community's quest for the atom bomb can be seen as a Grail quest also, with the Fisher King in this particular case being the appropriately crippled Franklin Roosevelt.

Through the debasement of myth, the color-coding of the Knights of the Round Table, and the literally explosive nature of his Grail, Barthelme is able in *The King* to lay bare the essential social, cultural, and political conflicts in Europe and America that began during World War II and continued throughout the following decades. By attacking modernism at the moment of that movement's demise, Barthelme implicates that failure in the rest of the century's cultural drift. Just as the Red Knight symbolizes Soviet communism and its continued influence throughout the twentieth century, the Black Knight symbolizes incipient African nationalism in a world freed from colonialism. The Grail that these knights seek — the Atom bomb — is revealed to be not a panacea for these divisions but merely a death-dealing apparatus that would simply exacerbate these pre-existing tensions. That Barthelme ends the novel with the atom bomb left undeveloped is perhaps his most telling comment on how the bomb affected twentieth century history. The U.S. and Japan barely appear in the novel, and yet it was the U.S.'s atomic bombings of Japan that ushered in the nuclear age. Through these omissions, Barthelme seems to be suggesting that by avoiding the use of the bomb, Europeans somehow managed to avoid making bad problems worse — at least for a short time.

Conclusion

Here is the end of the booke of kyng Arthur & of his noble
knyghtes of the rounde table that whan they were hole togy-
ders there was euer an C and xl and here is the ende of the
deth of Arthur ... [Malory *Corpus*].

The American fascination with the Arthurian cycle of mythol-
ogy continues. In the realm of literary fiction, David Foster Wallace, the
post-postmodernist writer who many critics view as the literary heir of
Thomas Pynchon himself, included in his 1999 volume of short stories,
Brief Interviews with Hideous Men, a story entitled "Tri-Stan: I Sold Sissee
Nar to Ecko." The piece is a clever retelling of several mythical tales,
including the Tristan and Isolde story, with the setting being "medieval"
California (B.C.—"Before Cable"), and Tri-Stan being a television production company headed by Agon M. Nar. Having wrested control of
Tri-Stan from Reggie Ecko, Mr. Nar proceeds to use his attractive daughter, Sissee, in advertisements, only to end up losing Sissee when she has
an affair with Ecko. Wallace leaves unanswered the question of whether
"it was just one of those large-r Romantic love-at-initial reception things,
the stuff of chivalric myth, the Tristian/ Launcelotian fuck-it-all plunge,
the Sicilian thunderbolt, the Wagnerian *Liebestod*," though the author
does concede that Ecko, in his diary, "represents himself as an Errant
Knight displaced from his proper place & time & embarked on your basic
demonic love-quest of chivalric Yore ..." (Wallace 210). Wallace presents
the tale via an aptly named narrator called Ovid, who sees the story as
representing "a kind of hottub-swingers' incest among Tristan &
Narcissus & Echo & Isolde ..." (Wallace 215). While Wallace's permuta-
tions on the Tristan and Isolde myth are admittedly bizarre, one thing
remains clear: the debasement of Arthurian myth continues.

No fewer than forty books on Arthurian themes were published in the United States in the year 2000 alone — a combination of new editions of old favorites, critical studies, and the standard works of pulp fantasy fiction, the genre in which Arthuriana has had its most lasting hold. More than a dozen films and television shows based on the Arthurian legends appeared during the 1990s. And with the untimely death of John F. Kennedy, Jr., on July 16, 1999, America and the world were deluged again with references to Camelot and the tragic legacy of the Kennedy family. Clearly Thomas Brown's observation that the promise of a return to Camelot was extinguished by Ted Kennedy's failed challenge for the 1980 Democratic nomination for the presidency was premature. Though John Kennedy *fils* had set out to distinguish himself in his mother's field — the world of publishing — he had never ruled out a life in politics, and more than a few Americans hoped that he someday would launch a political career. Just as they were robbed of seeing the potential of his father and uncles come to fruition, they also lost the hope of seeing the torch passed to the next generation.

Why do American writers and the American people remain fascinated by Arthur and the Knights of the Round Table? Certainly the United States, particularly since its emergence as a superpower, can no longer be said to be the "offspring" of Great Britain and thus have any greater attachment to England's national mythology than that of any other country. And as the cultural makeup of the United States continues to develop greater diversity and complexity, there is less reason for an "ethnic" connection to Arthuriana. Indeed, for many years, there have been more Americans of German ethnic descent than any other, but Americans have never felt the attraction to the *Nibelungenlied* that they have to the myth of Camelot, particularly as rendered by Malory and his imitators.

Perhaps the most compelling reason that Arthurian myth and legend has had such an enduring influence on American literature and culture is the myth's and the nation's own ties to Christianity. There is little question that Arthur is a sort of Christ figure, with even the account of his death and "afterlife" in Avalon leaving open the possibility that, as Christianity teaches about Jesus, he will one day return. After all, Arthur is, as T.H. White named him, "the once *and future* king." Even analyses of the Arthurian cycle that do not identify Arthur as a Christ figure cannot avoid the fact that the myth of Arthur is deeply steeped in medieval Christianity, with the quest for the Holy Grail being the central connection between the Bible and Malory (and the writers from whom he drew). In this paradigm, Arthur (or, depending on the rendering of the myth being read, the Fisher King) can be seen as personifying God and the Grail knight instead taking up the role of Christ. The comparison is particularly apt when the Grail knight is a chaste man such as Galahad or Perceval. And with the recovery of the relic, the king and the kingdom are reborn, suggesting something akin to the universal resurrection of the dead accomplished by Jesus' own resurrection. (Ryan *passim*)

In a country like the United States, with its overwhelmingly Christian majority, such Christian-tinged myths find fertile ground to engender more retellings of the story. Other works of literature or art may evoke uncomfortable questions about religion and faith in general, but the Arthurian cycle does not have that effect. Despite the fact that Martin Scorsese's 1988 film *The Last Temptation of Christ*, adapted from Nikos Kazantzakis' 1955 novel, is ultimately very affirmative of the Christian religion, it was nevertheless picketed and protested by Christian religious groups (many of whom refused to even view the film) who resented what they perceived to be a blasphemous characterization of Jesus. In a country where religious beliefs can become politicized in the realm of art, the choice of the Matter of Arthur is, in a sense, safer material for mass consumption because it does not undermine (either deliberately or in the view of consumers) heartfelt religious beliefs.

Of course, a good deal of the Arthurian material produced by serious writers of American fiction has consisted of inversions and perversions of the traditional story (David Foster Wallace's story being among the most recent examples). Thus there must necessarily follow a subsequent debasement of the Christian elements embedded in the myth. For example, if, for Pynchon and Barthelme, the Holy Grail has become a weapon of mass destruction, then what does this say about the significance of Christian relics and, therefore, Christianity? Are these authors' Grail characterizations slanted criticisms of the destructive aspects of organized religion? These are questions that have not been raised by faithful Christian readers of the works of those writers who have turned the myth on its head to suit political, social, or philosophical purposes. Indeed, it seems that Pynchon's use of profanity and explicit sexuality in *Gravity's Rainbow* raised far more eyebrows than did the replacement of the Holy Grail as the object of the quest with the V-2 rocket. The debased depiction of the Grail — the most tangible link to Christianity in the myth — went unnoticed, unlike the replacement of the chaste Grail knight with the promiscuous Slothrop.

The other principal reason that the Arthurian myth is so enduring in America is that it offers a prototype of leadership in the character of Arthur that can serve either as a role model or as an object of derision (or both). On the one hand, classic retellings of the Arthurian myth depict Camelot as the ideal kingdom, and it is therefore no wonder that a highly optimistic nation would choose to bestow the title of Camelot on the Kennedy White House. However, the Kennedy-Camelot link has proved to be a double-edged sword, as everyone from biographer and political analyst to tabloid journalist evokes Camelot while describing some embarrassing or lurid event in the lives of the Kennedys. For instance, Seymour Hersh's 1997 biography of JFK, which detailed his many extramarital affairs, was entitled *The Dark Side of Camelot*. Similarly, political dissident Noam Chomsky's 1993 analysis of Kennedy's Vietnam policy and its dire consequences was dubbed *Rethinking Camelot*. Clearly these writers are seeking to explode the Kennedy-Camelot connection that many Americans still hold in their minds; instead, they end up underscoring the connection by evoking Camelot in the first place, though their works may be truthful and valid.

But for a country that has never experienced life under even a titular monarchy, the Arthurian myth holds a certain fascination because it is something to which Americans cannot wholly relate. While it is has been shown that Kennedy, Franklin Roosevelt, and other U.S. presidents have garnered the respect and admiration (and contempt) usually reserved only for absolute rulers, in countries with monarchs, the relationship between the king (or queen) and the people is substantially different. During World War II, Great Britain and other constitutional monarchies that were occupied by the Axis powers found their populations rallying not around their prime ministers (though Winston Churchill did experience great popularity during the war), but around their monarchs. King Christian X of Denmark became a national symbol of resistance to Nazi occupation; King George VI made himself a visible symbol of the indefatigable spirit of the British people by appearing for photographs during the Blitz in front of bombed-out buildings.

Perhaps it is John Steinbeck, that most Arthurian-influenced of American authors, who best captures the nature of the American fascination with the Camelot myth. He writes in *Travels with Charley*, "We, as a nation, are as hungry for history as was England when Geoffrey of

Monmouth concocted his History of British Kings, many of whom he manufactured to meet the growing demand" (*Travels* 80-81). Steinbeck states the irrefutable truth that the United States, for a "Western" country, is a comparative *young* country. Having for the most part rejected the mythology of our continent's indigenous peoples, we are left having to create Johnny Appleseeds and Paul Bunyans to populate our national subconscious. But we are unable to conceive of a mythical figure to precede George Washington (or George W. Bush) in the way that Geoffrey could summon Arthur, Lear, and others as the predecessors of Alfred the Great (or Elizabeth II). There is no gray area for us before our recorded history. And so, Arthur fills our need for a mythical heritage — even if it is a heritage with which the United States broke official ties more than two centuries ago. King Arthur arrived on America's shores not long after that– and he is here to stay.

Bibliography

"America & the Americans." *National Steinbeck Center*. 1 Jan 2001 <*http://www. steinbeck.org/books&movies*>.

Arnold, Matthew. "Civilisation in the United States." *Complete Prose Works*. Vol. 10. Ed. R.H. Super. Ann Arbor, Mich.: U. Michigan Press, 1960. 489–504.

Astro, Richard. "Steinbeck's Bittersweet Thursday." Benson 204–15.

Baetzhold, Howard G. "The Composition of *A Connecticut Yankee*." Twain, *Connecticut Yankee* 342–60.

Barthelme, Donald. *The King*. New York: Harper & Row, 1990.

_____. "Not-Knowing." *Voicelust: Eight Contemporary Fiction Writers on Style*. Ed. Allen Weir. Lincoln, Neb.: U. Nebraska Press, 1985.

Beard, Daniel. *Hardly a Man Is Now Alive: The Autobiography of Dan Beard*. New York: Doubleday, 1939.

Bellamy, Joe David, and Pat Ensworth. "John Gardner." Chavkin 6–27.

Benson, Jackson J. *John Steinbeck, Writer: A Biography*. New York: Viking, 1984.

_____, ed. *The Short Novels of John Steinbeck: Critical Essays With a Checklist to Steinbeck Criticism*. Durham, N.C.: Duke UP, 1990.

Brans, Jo. "Embracing the World: An Interview With Donald Barthelme." *Southwest Review* 67.2 (1982): 121-37.

Brewer, Gay. *A Detective in Distress: Philip Marlowe's Domestic Dream*. Madison, Ind.: Brownstone, 1989.

Brown, Alan. "From Artist to Craftsman: Steinbeck's *Bombs Away*." Noble 213–22.

Brown, Thomas. *JFK: History of an Image*. Bloomington: Indiana UP, 1988.

Budd, Louis. "Uncle Sam." Twain *Connecticut Yankee* 401- 09.

Butts, Leonard. *The Novels of John Gardner: Making Life Art as a Moral Process*. Baton Rouge, La.: Louisiana State UP, 1988.

Cabell, James Branch. *Jurgen*. New York: Dover, 1977 (1922).

Campbell, Mary Baine. "Finding the Grail: Fascist Aesthetics and Mysterious Objects." Mancoff 213–25.

Chandler, Raymond. *The Big Sleep*. New York: Vintage, 1939.

_____. "Blackmailers Don't Shoot." (1933) *Red Wind: A Collection of Short Stories*. New York: World Publishing Co., 1946.

_____. *Chandler Before Marlowe*. Ed. Matthew J. Bruccoli. Foreword by Jacques Barzun. Columbia, S.C.: University of South Carolina Press, 1973.

_____. "The King in Yellow." (1938) *Simple* 84–138.

_____. *The Lady in the Lake*. New York: Vintage, 1992 (1943).

_____. "The Lady in the Lake." (1939) *Killer in the Rain*. New York: Ballantine, 1964. 288–337.

_____. *Raymond Chandler Speaking*. Ed. Dorothy Gardiner and Katherine Sorley Walker. Boston: Houghton, 1962.

_____. "Red Wind." (1938) *Trouble Is My Business*. New York: Vintage, 1992. 162–214.

_____. *Selected Letters of Raymond Chandler*. Ed. Frank MacShane. New York: Columbia UP, 1981.

_____. *The Simple Art of Murder*. New York: Vintage, 1988. (1950)

_____. "The Simple Art of Murder." *Simple* 1–18.

_____. "Smart-Aleck Kill." (1934) *Simple* 231–75.

Chavkin, Allan, ed. *Conversations with John Gardner*. Jackson, Miss.: UP of Mississippi, 1990.

Cowart, David. *Arches & Light: The Fiction of John Gardner*. Carbondale, Ill.: Southern Illinois UP, 1983.

Cox, James. "*A Connecticut Yankee in King Arthur's Court*: The Machinery of Self-Preservation." Twain, *Connecticut Yankee* 390–401.

Cunliffe, Marcus. "Mark Twain and his 'English' Novels." *Times Literary Supplement* 4108 (Dec. 25, 1981): 1503–04.

Diehl, Digby. "Medievalist in Illinois Ozarks." Chavkin 3–5.

Domini, John. "Donald Barthelme: The Modernist Uprising." *Southwest Review* 75.1 (1990): 95–112.

Eliot, T.S. *The Waste Land*. (1922) *The Norton Anthology of American Literature*. Vol. 2. Third Ed. Ed. Nina Baym et al. New York: Norton, 1989.

Emerson, Ralph Waldo. "Merlin" *Selections from Ralph Waldo Emerson*. Ed. Stephen E. Whicher. Boston: Houghton Mifflin, 1960. 447–50.

_____. "Poetry and Imagination." *Letters and Social Aims*. Ed. Edward W. Emerson. Boston: Houghton Mifflin, 1883. 7–75.

Everett, William A. "Images of Arthurian Britain in the American Musical Theater: *A Connecticut Yankee* and *Camelot*." *Sonneck Society for American Music Bulletin* 23.3 (1997). 1 Jan. 2001 <*http://www.american-music.org/bulletn/everett.htm*>.

Ferguson, Paul F., et al. "John Gardner: The Art of Fiction LXXIII." Chavkin 143–71.

Foner, Philip. *Mark Twain: Social Critic*. New York: International Publishers, 1958.

Fontana, Ernest. "Chivalry and Modernity in Raymond Chandler's *The Big Sleep*." *Western American Literature* 19.3 (1984): 179–86.

Fontenrose, Joseph. "*Tortilla Flat* and the Creation of a Legend." Benson 19–30.

Forbush, William Byron, and Dascomb Forbush. *The Knights of King Arthur: How to Begin and What to Do*. Oberlin, Ohio: The Knights of King Arthur, 1915.

Foster, Hal. *The Prince Valiant Companion*. Ed. Todd Goldberg et al. Mountain Home, Tenn.: Manuscript Press, 1992.

Fox-Friedman, Jeanne. "The Chivalric Order for Children: Arthur's Return in Late Nineteenth- and Early Twentieth-Century America." Mancoff 137–57.

French, Warren. *John Steinbeck*. New York: Twayne, 1961.

_____. *John Steinbeck's Fiction Revisited*. New York: Twayne, 1994.

_____. "Steinbeck's Use of Malory." Hayashi *Steinbeck* 4–11.

Gardner, John. "*The Acts of King Arthur and His Noble Knights* by John Steinbeck." *On Writers and Writing* 112–18.

_____. *The Alliterative Morte Arthure, the Owl and the Nightingale, and Five Other Middle English Poems in a Modernized Version with Comments on the Poems and Notes*. Carbondale, Ill.: Southern Illinois UP, 1971.

_____. *Freddy's Book*. New York: Vintage, 1980.

_____. "General Plan for *The Sunlight Dialogues*." *On Writers and Writing* 258–87.

_____. *Le Morte d'Arthur Notes*. Lincoln, Neb.: Cliff's Notes, 1967.

_____. *October Light*. New York: Vintage, 1989.

_____. *On Moral Fiction*. New York: Basic Books, 1977.

_____. *On Writers and Writing*. New York: Addison-Wesley, 1994.

_____. *The Resurrection*. New York: Ballantine, 1966.

_____. *The Sunlight Dialogues*. New York: Vintage, 1987.

Gentry, Curt. "John Steinbeck: America's Arthur Is Coming." *Conversations with John Steinbeck*. Thomas Fensch, ed. Oxford: Univ. of Mississippi Press, 1988.

Gregory, Lady Augusta. *Gods and Fighting Men*. New York: Oxford University Press, 1970 (1904).

Grella, George. "The Hard-Boiled Detective Novel." *Detective Fiction: A Collection of Critical Essays*. Ed. Robin W. Winks. Englewood Cliffs, N.J.: Prentice, 1980.

Hawthorne, Nathaniel. "The Antique Ring." *Eldritch Press*. 1 Jan. 2001 <*http://www.eldritchpress.org/nh/ar.html*>.

Hayashi, Tetsumaro, ed. *A New Study Guide to Steinbeck's Major Works, with Critical Explications*. Metuchen, N.J.: Scarecrow Press, 1993.

_____. *Steinbeck and the Arthurian Theme*. Muncie, Ind.: Ball State UP, 1975.

Hoben, John B. "So Much Divine Comedy." Twain, *Connecticut Yankee* 341-42.

Hodges, Laura F. "Arthur, Lancelot, and the Psychodrama of Steinbeck." *Steinbeck Quarterly* 13 (1980): 71- 79.

_____. "Steinbeck's Adaptation of Malory's Lancelot: A Triumph of Realism Over Supernaturalism." *Quondam et Futurus: A Journal of Arthurian Interpretations* 2.1 (1992): 69–81.

Hoffman, Andrew. *Inventing Mark Twain: The Lives of Samuel Langhorne Clemens*. New York: William Morris, 1997.

Howell, John M. *Understanding John Gardner*. Columbia, S.C.: Univ. of South Carolina Press, 1993.

Howells, William Dean. *My Mark Twain*. http://marktwain.miningco.com/library /texts/bl_wdh_mmt_ch007.htm (Feb. 1, 1999).

Hughes, Robert S., Jr. "'Some Philosophers in the Sun': Steinbeck's *Cannery Row*." Benson 119–31.

Kaplan, Justin. Introduction. *A Connecticut Yankee in King Arthur's Court*. By Mark Twain. New York: Penguin, 1986. 9–23.

Karl, Frederick. *American Fictions 1940/1980: A Comprehensive History and Critical Evaluation*. New York: Harper and Row, 1983.

Kennedy, John Fitzgerald. "Inaugural Address: 20 January 1961." *Inaugural Addresses of the Presidents of the United States From George Washington 1789 to George Bush 1989*. Washington: GPO, 1989.

Ketterer, David. "Epoch-Eclipse and Apocalypse: Special 'Effects' in *A Connecticut Yankee*." Twain, *Connecticut Yankee* 417–34.

Klein, Edward. "All Too Human: The Love Story of Jack and Jackie Kennedy." *Litrix Reading Room*. 1 Jan 2001 <*http://www.litrix.com/toohuman/toohu001. htm*>.

Lacy, Norris J. "King Arthur Goes to War." Mancoff 159–69.

Lanier, Sidney. *The Boy's Froissart*. New York: Scribner's, 1879.

_____. *The Boy's King Arthur*. New York: Scribner's, 1880.

Lawson, Lewis. "'Spiritually in Los Angeles': California Noir in *Lancelot*." *Southern Review* 24.4 (1988): 744–64.

Leitch, Thomas M. "Donald Barthelme and the End of the End." *Modern Fiction Studies* 28.1 (1982): 129–43.

Lerner, Alan Jay. *Camelot*. New York: Random House, 1961.

Levant, Howard. *The Novels of John Steinbeck: A Critical Study*. Columbia, Mo.: University of Missouri Press, 1974.

Lewis, Sinclair. *It Can't Happen Here*. New York: Signet, 1993.

Lojek, Helen. "Steinbeck's *In Dubious Battle* (1936)." Hayashi *Guide* 115–38.

Loomis, Roger Sherman. *The Development of Arthurian Romance*. New York: Norton, 1963.

Lupack, Alan. "The Figure of Arthur in America." Mancoff 121-36.

Lynn, Kenneth S. "The Volcano." Twain, *Connecticut Yankee* 383–89.

Malory, Thomas. *Le Morte d'Arthur*. 2 vols. New York: Penguin, 1969 (William Caxton, ed. 1485).

_____. *Le Morte d'Arthur* (H. Oskar Sommer, ed. 1889). *Corpus of Middle English Prose and Verse*. 1 Jan 2001 <*http://www.hti.umich.edu/cgi/c/cme/cme-idx?type = header&idno=MaloryWks2*>.

Mancoff, Debra N., ed. *King Arthur's Modern Return*. New York: Garland, 1998.

Marling, William. *Raymond Chandler*. Boston: Twayne, 1986.

McCaffery, Larry. "Barthelme's *Snow White*: The Aesthetics of Trash." *Critique: Studies in Modern Fiction* 16.3 (1975): 19–32.

McWilliams, Dean. *John Gardner*. Boston: Twayne, 1990.

Messent, Peter. "Towards the Absurd: Mark Twain's *A Connecticut Yankee in King Arthur's Court*, *Pudd'n'Head Wilson* and *The Great Dark*." *Mark Twain: A Sumptuous Variety*. Ed. Robert Giddings. Totowa, N.J.: Barnes & Noble, 1985. 176–98.

Meyer, Michael J. "Steinbeck's *The Winter of Our Discontent* (1961)." Hayashi *Guide* 240–73.

Morace, Robert A. "New Fiction, Popular Fiction, and John Gardner's Middle/Moral Way." Morace and VanSpanckeren 130–45.

_____, and Kathryn VanSpanckeren, eds. *John Gardner: Critical Perspectives*. Carbondale, Ill.: Southern Illinois UP, 1982.

Morris, Gregory L. "A Babylonian in Batavia: Mesopotamian Literature and Lore in *The Sunlight Dialogues*." Morace and VanSpanckeren 28–45

_____. *A World of Order and Light: The Fiction of John Gardner*. Athens, Ga.: Univ. of Georgia Press, 1984.

Naipaul, V.S. *The Overcrowded Barracoon*. London: Andre Deutsch, 1972.

Natov, Roni, and Geraldine DeLuca. "An Interview with John Gardner." Chavkin 99–116.

Noble, Donald R., ed. *The Steinbeck Question: New Essays in Criticism.* Troy, N.Y.: Whitston Publishing Co., 1993.

Owens, Louis. "Critics and Common Denominators: Steinbeck's *Sweet Thursday.*" Benson 195–203.

Paine, Albert Bigelow. "His Literary Best and Worst." Twain *Connecticut Yankee* 337–42.

Parini, Jay. *John Steinbeck: A Biography.* New York: Henry Holt, 1995.

Pelley, William Dudley. *Cripples' Money: Who Gets the Proceeds of the Presidential Birthday Balls?* Asheville, N.C.: Pelley Publishers, n.d.

_____. *The Door to Revelation: An Autobiography.* Asheville, N.C.: Pelley Publishers, 1939.

_____. *My Seven Minutes in Eternity with Their Aftermath.* Noblesville, Ind.: Fellowship Press, 1971.

_____. *Twilight Clear: A Volume of Soulcraft Poems.* Noblesville, Ind.: W.D. Pelley, 1961. n.pag.

_____, and Clarence Brown. *The Light of Faith.* Dir. Clarence Brown. Perf. Lon Chaney, Hope Hampton, and E.K. Lincoln. 1922. Videocassette. Sinister Cinema, n.d.

Percy, Walker. *Lancelot.* New York: Ivy Books, 1977.

Prindle, Dennis. "The Pretexts of Romance: Steinbeck's Allegorical Naturalism from *Cup of Gold* to *Tortilla Flat.*" Noble 23–36.

Pynchon, Thomas. *Gravity's Rainbow.* New York: Penguin, 1973.

Rabinovitz, Dina. "Music That Hath Charms for Hitler." *The Irish Times* July 4, 1998. http://www.irish- times.com/irish-times/paper/1998/0704/fea7.html (July 5, 1999).

Rahv, Philip. "Paleface and Redskin." *Image and Idea: Twenty Essays on Literary Themes.* New York: New Directions, 1957. 1-6.

"The Real Mark Twain." *Literary Digest* 17 (Sept. 24, 1898). http://markt-wain.tqn. com/library/texts/bl_real_mt.htm (Feb. 1, 1999).

Reilly, Charlie. "A Conversation with John Gardner." Chavkin 50–83.

Ribuffo, Leo P. *The Old Christian Right: The Protestant Far Right from the Great Depression to the Cold War.* Philadelphia: Temple University Press, 1983.

Rogers, Rodney O. "Twain, Taine, and Lecky: The Genesis of a Passage in *A Connecticut Yankee.*" *Modern Language Quarterly* 34 (1973): 436–37.

Ryan, Steven. "Le héros se divinise: Le voyage spirituel et symbolique de Perceval dans, 'Le conte de graal' de Chrétien de Troyes." Unpublished essay, Dept. of French, West Chester University, West Chester, PA, 2000.

Sargent, Mary L. "A Connecticut Yankee in Jane Lampton's South: Mark Twain and the Regicide." *Mississippi Quarterly* 40.1 (Winter 1986–87): 21- 31.

Scott, Irving M. "The Mission of the Knights of Labor." *Overland Monthly and Out West Magazine* 9.53 (May 1887): 471-82.

Shakespeare, William. *King Lear. William Shakespeare: The Complete Works.* Ed. Alfred Harbage. New York: Viking, 1969.

Shanley, Mary Lyndon, and Peter G. Stillman. "Mark Twain: Technology, Social Change, and Political Power." in *The Artist and Political Values.* Ed. Benjamin Barber and Michael McGrath. New Brunswick, N.J.: Transaction, 1982. TK-TK.

Simmonds, Roy S. "A Note on Steinbeck's Unpublished Arthurian Stories."

Steinbeck and the Arthurian Theme, Testumaro Hayashi, ed., Muncie, Indiana: Ball State UP, 1975. 25–29.

_____. "The Unrealized Dream: Steinbeck's Modern Version of Malory." *Steinbeck and the Arthurian Theme*, Testumaro Hayashi, ed., Muncie, Indiana: Ball State UP, 1975. 30–43.

Simpson, Hassell A. "'A Butcher's Thumb': Oral-Digital Consciousness in *The Big Sleep* and Other Novels of Raymond Chandler." *Journal of Popular Culture* 23.1 (1991): 83–92.

Slotkin, Richard. "The Hard-Boiled Detective Story: From the Open Range to the Mean Streets." *The Sleuth and the Scholar: Origins, Evolution, and Current Trends in Detective Fiction.* Ed. Barbara A. Rader and Howard G. Zettler. New York: B. Greenwood, 1988.

Smith, Henry Nash. *Mark Twain: The Development of a Writer.* Cambridge, Mass: Harvard UP, 1962.

_____. *Mark Twain's Fable of Progress: Political and Economic Ideas in* A Connecticut Yankee. New Brunsick, N.J.: Rutgers UP, 1964.

Speir, Jerry. *Raymond Chandler.* New York: Ungar, 1981.

Spenser, Sir Edmund. *The Faerie Queen*

_____. *The Faerie Queen: Books I to III.* London: Everyman's Library, 1987.

Steele, Timothy. "The Structure of the Detective Story: Classical or Modern?" *Modern Fiction Studies* 27.4 (1981-82): 555–70.

Steinbeck, Elaine, and Robert Wallsten, eds. *Steinbeck: A Life in Letters.* New York: Viking, 1975, and Penguin, 1989.

Steinbeck, John. *The Acts of King Arthur and His Noble Knights: From the Winchester Manuscripts of Thomas Malory and Other Sources.* New York: Noonday, 1976.

_____. *America and Americans.* New York: Viking, 1966.

_____. *Bombs Away: The Story of a Bomber Team.* New York: Paragon House, 1990 (1942).

_____. *Cannery Row.* New York: Penguin, 1994 (1945).

_____. *Cup of Gold.* New York: Penguin, 1995 (1929).

_____. "Dreams Piped from Cannery Row." *New York Times* Nov. 27, 1955, sec. 2: 1+.

_____. *In Dubious Battle.* (1936) *Novels* 529–794.

_____. *Novels and Stories 1932–1937.* New York: Library of America, 1994.

_____. *Sweet Thursday.* New York: Penguin, 1996 (1954).

_____. *Tortilla Flat.* (1935) *Novels* 369–528.

_____. *Travels with Charley: In Search of America.* New York: Penguin, 1962.

_____. *The Winter of Our Discontent.* New York: Bantam, 1961.

Sublett, Bruce L. "Archetypes and Patterns of the Grail Romance in Thomas Pynchon's *Gravity's Rainbow.*" M.A. Thesis Stephen F. Austin State U., 1986.

Timmerman, John H. *John Steinbeck's Fiction: The Aesthetics of the Road Taken.* Norman, Okla.: Univ. of Oklahoma Press, 1986.

Twain, Mark. *The Autobiography of Mark Twain.* Ed. Charles Neider. New York: Harper, 1990.

_____. *A Connecticut Yankee in King Arthur's Court.* Ed. Alison Endor. New York: Norton, 1985.

_____. Letter to the President of Yale University. June 1888. *Hartford Courant.* http://www.courant.com/news/special/twain/yale.htm (Feb. 1, 1999).

_____. *Mark Twain's Notebooks and Journals.* Ed Frederick Anderson et al. Berkeley, Calif.: University of California Press, 1975.

_____. "The New Dynasty." *Tales, Sketches, Speeches, and Essays 1852–1890.* Ed. Louis J. Budd. New York: Library of America, 1992. 883–90.

_____. *The Prince and the Pauper.* New York: Bantam, 1991.

_____, and William Dean Howells. *Mark Twain — Howells Letters: The Correspondence of Samuel L. Clemens and William D. Howells, 1872–1910.* Vol. 2. Ed. Henry Nash Smith et al. Cambridge, Mass: Harvard UP, 1960.

Updike, John. *Brazil.* New York: Knopf, 1994.

_____. "Four Sides of One Story." *The Music School.* New York: Vintage, 1980. 87–100.

Verduin, Kathleen. *Studies in Medievalism.* 1 February 2001. <http://www.hope.edu/academic/english/perspages/verduin/homepage.html>.

Wallace, David Foster. "Tri-Stan: I Sold Sissee Nar to Ecko." *Brief Interviews With Hideous Men.* Boston: Little, Brown and Company, 1999. 200–17

Weir, Robert E. *Beyond Labor's Veil: The Culture of the Knights of Labor.* State College, Pa.: Pennsylvania State UP, 1996.

Weisenburger, Steven. *A Gravity's Rainbow Companion: Sources & Contexts for Pynchon's Novel.* Athens, Ga.: U. Georgia Press, 1988.

Williams, James D. "Revision and Intention in Mark Twain's *A Connecticut Yankee.*" Twain, *Connecticut Yankee* 361-68.

Williams, Mary C. "Lessons from Ladies in Steinbeck's 'Gawain, Ewain, and Marhalt." *Avalon to Camelot* 1.4 (1984): 40–41.

Winther, Per. *The Art of John Gardner: Instruction and Exploration.* Albany, N.Y.: State Univ. of New York Press, 1992.

Wolfe, Peter. *Something More Than Night: The Case of Raymond Chandler.* Bowling Green, Ohio: Bowling Green University Popular Press, 1985.

Index